LOVE IN AN AGE OF UNCER...

Jocelyn Chaplin is a psychotherapist, artist and co-founder of The Serpent Institute, a centre for Goddess spirituality and personal development. She has a particular interest in developing the rhythm model as an alternative to hierarchical ways of thinking and being. These ideas are explored on a psychological level in her previous book FEMINIST COUNSELLING IN ACTION. She has led many courses and workshops on the Goddess, Psychology and Mythology, Counselling and Therapy, and Alternative Politics, and in addition has a private practice in West London. Jocelyn grew up in West Africa and has travelled widely visiting ancient sites relevant to Goddess spirituality including Malta, Gozo, and Greece. These have provided inspiration for her painting and writing. She has had several exhibitions of her work at various venues including the Ecology Centre Gallery.

LOVE IN AN AGE OF UNCERTAINTY

Reclaiming Aphrodite

Jocelyn A. Chaplin

Aquarian/Thorsons
An Imprint of HarperCollins*Publishers*

The Aquarian Press
An Imprint of HarperCollins*Publishers*
77—85 Fulham Palace Road,
Hammersmith, London W6 8JB

Published by The Aquarian Press 1993
1   3   5   7   9   10   8   6   4   2

A catalogue record for this book
is available from the British Library

ISBN 1 85538 169 9

Phototypeset by Harper Phototypesetters Limited,
Northampton, England
Printed in Great Britain by
Hartnolls Ltd., Bodmin, Cornwall

*This book is dedicated to my
daughter Rosita*

Contents

Acknowledgements

I would especially like to thank all those women and men who have shared their journeys with me in one way or another: all my students and colleagues at the Serpent Institute, Maccabi and Mary Ward Centres; my clients, friends and lovers; and of course, my daughter, Rosita. So many people have helped me indirectly with this book I can't give everyone's name, but would like to mention Annie, Chantel, Melanie, Kostas, Kaz, Richard and Peter. I particularly want to thank the other members of the 'Reclaiming Aphrodite' Women Artists' Group: Marianne Sawyer, Meena Jaffrey, Fiona Graham and Cilla Conway.

Special thanks to Mary Clemmey, my agent, without whose support and encouragement this book would probably never have been published, and to Marion Russell and Liz Puttick, my editors at HarperCollins. I also want to thank Anne Gilbert for typing it so well and so quickly.

Goddess Spirituality

We are living in times of great uncertainty, in which all the safe old structures are crumbling around us. Not only are the all-embracing systems such as communism and Christianity disappearing, but so are all the old absolute truths and beliefs about relationships, sex, marriage and gender. Even things like the 'rules for dating' seem to be changing almost daily. Yet for many people, encouraged by the media, the area of love and romance seems to be the one certainty in this age of chaos.

But what do we mean by 'love'? In contemporary Western society it is usually immediately associated with romance. People think of a couple, generally young, 'in love', as portrayed in the movies. At the time of writing, the ideal romantic couple would be Tom Cruise and Nicole Kidman. Yesterday there was the fairy-tale marriage of Prince Charles and Princess Diana, straight out of the picture books — perfect — or was it? Now we read about the human truth underneath that particular myth.

Society tends to create the myths it needs to keep itself as it is (or was). But a time of change also needs its myths, to make sense of what is actually happening and to help the move towards a better future. Today's romantic myths may not be helping social change and may also encourage a very limited concept of what love is. But what do we put in their place? What kinds of myths will help rather than hinder the change

towards greater equality, fairness, tolerance and joy in living
— changes that many, if not most people would like to see?

As a psychotherapist I daily witness the damaging effects
romantic mythology has on clients' relationships and lives,
creating endless dissatisfaction and lack of joy in the present.
I listen to people questioning all their old beliefs and
assumptions, but still wanting *something*, some framework,
some meaning and, of course, love.

This deep questioning of old truths is no longer carried out
only by a few mystics or philosophers. More and more of us
are realizing that those so-called truths were not god-given,
but created by human beings in the first place. This can be hard
for us to take. It can feel as if the very ground beneath us has
turned to shifting sands that threaten to engulf us completely.
This uncertainty exists not only in philosophical treatises, but
in the minds of every parent who is no longer sure how to
bring up their children, or the ordinary person unsure of how
to relate to the opposite sex.

God no longer has all the answers, nor does mummy or
daddy or teacher. Even science and reason seem to have failed.
The twentieth century's 'god' of reason, which was supposed
to have taken over from the old man in the sky, has not after
all solved the problems of the world. He is a cold god, unable
to satisfy the deep urges in the human soul to connect directly
with the energies of the universe. People ask, 'Where is love,
in this world of reason? Where is the wisdom of the heart to
complement the knowledge of the head? Where is the richness
of myth and symbolism?'

For many non-religious people, the one connection they feel
with those universal energies is in the experience of love,
especially 'falling in love'. Falling in love is seen as a 'problem'
by far too many people, including psychologists. The 'ecstatic'
side of life has been devalued, denied or distorted, not only
by 'moral majorities', but by many therapists and 'new age'
thinkers. What we need now, therefore, are new myths of love
and ecstasy, of sex and spirituality, to take us forward, rather
than backward to the old social structures that are upheld

through outdated stories of perfect couples, perfect families and perfect people. This book explores some new but also some very old myths and ways of thinking about love.

If we see all our belief systems as myths in some way or another, then the question no longer arises as to what is truth and what is myth. Rather we need to ask which myths are *useful* for empowering people, for the survival of the planet and for social change, and which myths are no longer useful. There is contradiction and paradox in this approach. On the one hand there are no absolute truths, but on the other we need some frameworks and myths to believe in as if they were true. And on one hand we no longer believe that the old certainties were literally handed down to us by God, but on the other most of us still believe in some kind of God or higher power, or even simply a hidden order to life. Finally, while questioning the concepts we have in our *minds*, there is an increasing valuing of our *bodies* and of nature. Perhaps the experiences of our bodies and the cycles of nature — birth, growth, death — are all that we can be certain of.

Yet out of all these contradictions are growing new spiritual and psychological ways of thinking and being that may provide a deeper and ultimately more satisfying meaning for living and loving than the Hollywood myths. The approach explored in this book I call goddess spirituality. But that too is just a metaphor that can be used if useful and discarded if not.

Goddess spirituality is very flexible and takes many forms. Although it has largely developed over the past 20 years as part of the women's movement, especially in the USA, it is part of a much older tradition, remnants of which survive in most native cultures around the world. These remnants are usually described as Pagan or nature worshipping. It is connected to the green movement, eco-feminism and creation spirituality, and there are some specific traditions, such as Wicca, that come under its 'umbrella'. But in this book I am going to take a very general approach to goddess spirituality, one that is deliberately *not* based on any one tradition, that is for men as

well as women and is not a new religion or a set of blueprints
for living. It is simply an approach to life that has been useful
to myself and many others.

There are many levels on which we can experience the
goddess. These are described in more detail in Chapter 1,
which uses the image of a spiral to portray the goddess in all
her aspects. The first aspect resembles what most of us think
of as God — the source, the life force, the spirit within matter,
the order within chaos, the rhythm of life. The goddess is not
something outside nature, but a part of it. Another aspect is
Mother Nature, sometimes personified as Gaia, which was her
ancient Greek name. Calling nature a goddess can help us to
respect her more deeply and to try to live more in harmony
with her ecological balancing mechanisms, her cycles and her
rhythms. It can help us to recognise that nature is sacred. Of
course, neither God nor nature is either female or male in terms
of gender, but it seems useful at this point in history to put
female imagery onto the divine. It can be seen as a rebalancing
process after 5,000 years of patriarchy — literally, the 'rule of
the fathers'.

Goddess spirituality sees as sacred the parts of nature that
are our human bodies. All bodies can be seen as temples for
her sacred energy, not just 'perfect' bodies. Today there is so
much emphasis on the external image of our bodies that
millions have become obsessed with dieting, body building,
and so on, instead of fully living *inside* their bodies. All of us
are goddesses and gods, whatever we look like.

Goddess spirituality sees humans as intimately interconnected with the rest of nature, and values our bodies'
responses to the environment, whether they are pain, anger or
joy. These feelings do not need to be repressed in order for us
to be fully spiritual, as they do in many patriarchal religions.

In goddess spirituality today, as I see it, there is a strong
emphasis on therapy and counselling to help clear out the
emotional responses that we learned in our pasts which have
got stuck and are therefore blocking our ability to respond
appropriately in the present. Therapy and counselling can help

us to dissolve unhelpful ways of thinking and prevent us from identifying too much with our egos. At the same time they can help us develop a strong centre within, from which to watch and delight in the dances of our many selves, many feelings and many thoughts.

Goddess spirituality recognizes and works with the 'dark' side of life as well as the 'light'. Based on nature's cycles of, for example, day turning into night, it makes this approach feel natural. Unless we fully experience and express our anger there is no space for deep joy. People may even have to visit the 'underworld' in their spiritual journeys in order to face deep pains, rages or fears within themselves. This is the modern equivalent of the journey of initiation undertaken by the shaman or seer of old, which often involved a symbolic death.

The spirituality of the goddess is also, and perhaps most basically, about living in love, living ecstatically (without drugs), experiencing pleasure as divine. It does not restrict the feeling of being in love to a few years, months or weeks of being with one other human individual, but sees it as our birthright, how we are meant to live all the time, except when pain or rage are natural, appropriate responses to events. Sexual, erotic, love energy is seen as sacred and a vital link with the primal energies of the universe as experienced by the human body. All forms of genuine love, including sexual love, are seen as goddess energy to be used in service to her, rather than to gain power or control.

This spirituality has different frameworks of thinking that help people live in a way that is fuller, more human and more loving. At present, patriarchal thinking is hierarchical and goal orientated. Even in relationships and sex there is generally the thought that one person is superior or that control must be maintained. There is also the idea that there are rigid set goals such as marriage or orgasm towards which everything is geared. This is linear thinking, which is necessary sometimes but not all the time, and perhaps especially not in our human relationships. Instead we use the models of spirals and rhythms in which there is a constant flow between opposites, backwards and forwards, up and down, in and out. We can be both strong *and* vulnerable, joyful *and* sad, extrovert *and* introvert, although usually at different times. We can 'go with the flow' and trust the process of life, rather than use our need for control to take us in one set direction for ever.

In this world-view, daily life is as important as 'spiritual' events. There is an emphasis on living in the present. We can make anything we do sacred by giving it all our focused attention and love. If specific rituals are carried out they tend to be more spontaneous and personal than in most other traditions, and are often linked to psychological understandings. Symbols and images have fluid rather than rigid meanings.

Within goddess spirituality there are positive and varied images of the divine female to empower women in a society where most female images are limited, stereotyped and inferior to men. This book explores several of them, but also looks at some male images as well. Men too need to get away from stereotypes. Since classical Greek thinking still provides the framework for Western civilization, most of the images and myths in the book are taken from ancient Greece and then changed in order to make them more useful for today. I also explore some African and ancient British myths and images.

Interwoven with the myths are personal stories taken from my own experience and from that of friends and clients (with details changed), as we search for meaning and self-discovery in these times of transition. Both the myths and the personal stories can shed light on and give purpose to our individual journeys. There are explorations of personal transition times, such as from youth to adulthood and from young adulthood to mid-life. Finally there is a description of a Utopian society based on these non-hierarchical, rhythmic frameworks, showing how goddess spirituality could work in everyday life.

1

Reclaiming Aphrodite

A NEW MYTHOLOGY OF LOVE

Everyone wants love. But exactly what each person means by that elusive little word depends on their belief system. That one word has more meanings and myths surrounding it than most others in the English language. To begin with, many people think of love as a thing to get or possess, like everything else in our consumer society: an object to be kept and used to enhance the status of its owner. It is seen to come only from another person, not from inside oneself or from a whole range of connections with others and with nature itself.

The ecstasy of falling in love generally lasts for a tragically short period of time, and yet this is for many their only time of experiencing being fully alive and in touch with the life force. When this fades the ensuing disappointment often gets blamed on the other person, who is sometimes seen as taking 'it' away or ceasing to inspire 'it'. Some live life in a constant state of quiet dissatisfaction inside or outside partnership relationships, including marriage. Others search for the experience of ecstasy and connection through drugs or other addictions.

It seems that a sense of ultimate aloneness is just too much for most people to bear, unless they have a religious framework of some kind. The modern myth tells us that this 'alone' feeling will go away only when we find the perfect partner, to be 'kept' for as long as possible, preferably forever.

It also tells us that this partner must be an adult with whom there is or could be a sexual relationship. It does not mean a relationship with friends, children, colleagues or neighbours, for example. At least today it does not always insist on marriage or heterosexuality. But the image of the equal, loving couple is very powerful. This is what the myth says: 'In the midst of all this confusion and the breakdown of old certainties, the one thing you can rely on is love. But this is a very particular sort of love. It is the love for and from that one-and-only special person who is your soul mate. They alone can rescue you from this aloneness and uncertainty. And then when you are a solid, united *couple* you can stand together against the rest of the world.'

Even therapists often collude with this myth, while often recognizing that in a sense everyone is actually looking for their mother! People want to be accepted with unconditional love, the kind of love they experienced from their mothers when they were babies, but most of all they want that love to come from their one-and-only other. This myth does not encourage a communal or generally caring way of life. Perhaps it is no longer a very useful myth. Yet it is deeply ingrained, and not only in fairy stories about women being rescued by Prince Charming or a knight in shining armour; or, for men, in the story of Beauty and the Beast or in the dream of finding the perfect doll or mother figure.

Underneath all the myths about finding the perfect partner is a story from classical patriarchal Greece, so often the source of our ideas. It was first told by Plato, and goes something like this: 'Once upon a time all people had two heads and four arms and four legs and were blissfully happy and contented. But they began to misbehave and so one of the gods decided to split them all in half as a punishment. This created the kinds of humans that we have today. But from the moment we were split, we have all been searching for our "other half", our one-and-only perfect partner.'

The recent *Hite Report on Women and Love* in America reveals the depth to which this myth remains, even in a society where there has been so much recent emphasis on becoming 'whole people' individually. The longing for union with the beloved may stem from a deeper, more spiritual level, which we shall explore later, but in the minds of most modern Western women and men it still means one other human adult (usually a sexual partner) with whom you should be able to 'share everything'. Hite found that while most (84 per cent) of the women she surveyed put love relationships of this kind at the top of their priorities in life, few of them (less than one in five) had found the love they were looking for. And within the relationships that they did have, a horrifying 96 per cent felt that they were giving more emotional support than they were getting. So for a lot of women the myth certainly is not being lived in reality and may even be contributing to the dissatisfaction so many feel with their relationships. It is interesting to note that the very word relationship has now generally come to mean only a particular kind of relationship between two sexually interested adults.

The book *Women Who Love Too Much* was a surprise best seller in the 1980s. But while questioning many of the myths surrounding love relationships, it does not go that step further to reconstruct a more useful myth about love. Women in that book are generally advised to stop falling in love and giving away all their power to unappreciative men. Good advice, but then it is suggested that they find sensible men instead and settle into sensible couple relationships and give up craving excitement.

I would like to suggest an alternative myth that doesn't devalue the power of that ecstatic energy we also call being in love. This myth goes as follows: 'We are all born tingling with love energy all over our bodies and interconnected with the similar energies in the universe around us. This is like a state of being in love. It is our natural birthright. It is how we were 'meant to be' all the time, feeling everything intensely and ecstatically. Sometimes other people or situations help to inspire these feelings, but they do not totally depend on one or more other people. This love energy actually belongs to us.

It isn't possible to 'love too much' because that is simply being fully alive. We can channel this energy towards others: lovers, friends, children and strangers, or even trees. Or it can be focused back into our own bodies and used as healing energy or to enhance our sensual enjoyment of life. This energy can be like pure, golden light, or it can be divided into Eros, which is erotic love energy, and Agape, which is compassionate love energy. Both kinds are equally important.'

This myth does not limit love to couple relationships but includes all the relationships that we have, with people, with parts of ourselves and with nature herself. This is not a new myth; indeed, it may be one of the oldest of all, understood by human societies for thousands of years before patriarchal marriage systems and stories about the evils of the body, and especially sexuality, began to be believed as truths. Yet, despite their largely patriarchal nature, most world religions have somewhere in their more mystical teachings some under-standing of the sacredness of ecstasy, of erotic as well as compassionate love. From the Sufis to the Gnostics, from Hindu Tantrism to Pagan Wicca this wisdom has been developed. What I hope to do in this book is to put it in a modern, everyday social and psychological, as well as spiritual, context.

This primal love energy is what I mean by the goddess, and when we feel ecstatically 'in love' we are experiencing her or it (the goddess is essentially genderless) most directly. It is in everything, it accepts everything and connects everything, which to me feels more like the unconditional love of a mother than the more judging love of the patriarchal father. While the energy itself has no gender, when humans experience it indirectly through images and myths it can get distorted through our social, gendered perceptions and hierarchies. I therefore describe this love as the goddess rather than as god, with all the inevitable male associations, in order to help us get away from the masculine hierarchies of most religions. Love is not a thing given by a separate being at the top of some spiritual ladder, but is already in everything and everyone. Yet there are many levels of reality, and the goddess transforms into many forms, from the unseen rhythms of nature to the smile on a baby's face.

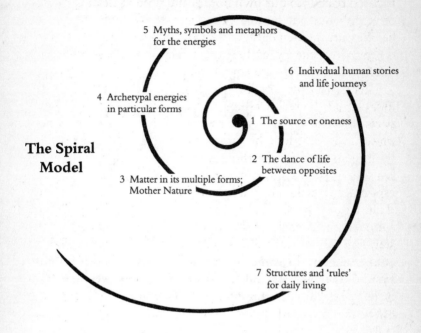

The Spiral Model

In order to clarify how this love energy, the energy of the goddess, manifests in the world, I have devised a seven-part spiral model that I have found useful in my teaching and in my own self-development. I describe what each aspect on the spiral means in terms of our human experience, both individually and collectively at this time of social upheaval.

The spiral shape follows the natural form of life processes much more than the more familiar, hierarchical structure of most of our models of analysis. So we start in the centre rather than at the top or bottom. The spiralling, ever-changing process is itself what we might call goddess or nature or creation. But we need to divide it as mythologies have always done for the sake of our limited human understanding. The spiral model shows us the mythology of goddess spirituality, which is explored in more detail in subsequent chapters of this book.

Aspect 1: The Source

At the centre, the goddess is *the source* from which everything is formed. She is pure energy, golden light. She is everything and everything is her. She is the oneness from which all forms divide. She is pure love.

The human experience of her is a sense of oneness with everything, a melting into golden energy, a feeling of pure bliss. In such a state we are experiencing the essence of the goddess.

Aspect 2: The Dance of Opposites

She divides into primal opposites of pushing and pulling, desire and repulsion, and *becomes the dance* between them. She is the pulsating rhythm that weaves through the universe between its many polarities. She is what the ancient Chinese called the Tao, the process of change itself, and she is the dialectic principle. She is Rhea, the flow; she is Eurynome, the wide-wandering one; she is Eros, the dance of desire and interconnection. She is the sacred serpent, the primal life force itself. She is the process of the goddess becoming manifest.

We can understand her intellectually as relations between opposites, or intuitively feel her and listen out for her 'words' of wisdom in our bellies. We can live life to flow with her rather than against her. We can learn to 'trust the process' and be receptive to what life has to teach us. We can live fully in the here and now.

Aspect 3: Matter in its Multiple Forms

She divides again and again and again, and material forms as we see them are created, grow, die and are recreated. She becomes our bodies and other natural forms. She is Gaia, the Earth mother. She is Yemaya, the sea mother. She is womb and she is tomb. She is flesh and she is the cooking-pot.

The human experience of her is our bodies, female and male, old and young. We feel her energy tingling through our limbs. We live in our bodies. We love these changing forms that her energy has taken. We learn to ground ourselves in our bodies and accept them. We enjoy and express our sexuality as an expression of her and as celebration of divine energy.

Aspect 4: Archetypal Energies

Her forms take on different qualities of energy — archetypal energies. She is fiery, inspirational energy. She is raging energy. She is gentle, watery energy. She is sensitive and emotional. She is bright, intellectual energy, airy and lofty. She is earthy, grounded, practical energy. She is compassion. She is wisdom. She is knowledge. She is organization.

She is fourfold and she is threefold. She is the trinity of Virgin, Mother and Crone: Kore, Demeter and Hecate. She is the waxing, full, waning and dark of the moon. She is the developing, the peaking and the consolidating of all processes and projects. She can be sevenfold, as in the seven planets of the ancient world, she can be ninefold, she can be any number of the infinite aspects of nature, of life.

We recognize her through images of archetypal energies. These images are mediated by the particular societies and periods of history in which people live. The energies can be represented by goddesses and gods, heroines and heroes, and these can help us to experience a whole range of feelings and sides of ourselves. We can be both Artemis *and* Aphrodite, Hermes *and* Zeus, albeit usually at different times. Astrology, the Tarot and other systems that capture the archetypes in their symbols can be useful in understanding ourselves and giving meaning to our own personal stories and journeys. We may feel that in this lifetime, in this particular form, at this particular time, we have certain tasks, certain energies that are uniquely ours. We may even identify greatly with one specific kind of energy or archetype in order to be most fully ourselves. Or we may need to balance one energy against another if we have become too identified with one archetype. Goddess spirituality in this aspect primarily involves being authentic, expressing all our potential and balancing our energies.

Aspect 5: Myths, Symbols and Metaphors

In this aspect the archetypal energies are given social form and meaning. This is the place where human imagination (greatly affected by particular social and economic conditions at particular times in history) connects with those energies. Unlike Jung I don't believe that archetypal forms are timeless and universal, only the relatively formless energies behind them. The human body and its processes may be universal, but the meanings we give them are not. They are largely socially constructed.

Goddess spirituality has its own set of myths and images that are particularly relevant for today. Many appear to be arising spontaneously from artists and writers who may not even think of themselves as spiritual. Some people are deliberately rejecting patriarchal imagery for the goddess alternative. Others say that the divine feminine is at last returning to humankind as an imagery badly needed in the unbalanced, over-'masculinized' world of today. From visions of the Virgin Mary to the increased interest in Wicca or witchcraft, the metaphor of the goddess awakening is a powerful one.

Love can be represented in ways that empower rather than objectify women. Images of powerful Earth-mother love, lesbian and gay love, love between friends and women joyously expressing their own sexuality with or without others are all important. Myths and images of men also enjoying their sexuality without oppressing others, and playing caring fathering roles, are also important. A range of images for people to choose from and move flexibly between is important for progressive social change towards equality and for expressing our capacity to love. This level is about fully human aspects of the goddess and belongs to the collective mythology.

In the goddess spirituality there are many forms that the new myths and rituals take. For example, there are group pilgrimages to sacred sites of either natural or human-created kinds. As well as formal, organized groups such as the Wicca covens, thousands of women and men gather in therapy workshops or informal groups to do nature-based rituals, for example at full moons.

Aspect 6: Individual Stories and Life Journeys

At this particular point in history it seems that many people are following their own individual journeys towards spiritual truths and experiences rather than sticking to an existing religion. Perhaps each age has its specific religious needs. Today the idea of a God revealing absolute truths to select groups of people might not be a useful myth. People want to find their own truths. This may involve taking bits out of various religions as well as using our own feelings and experiences. The goddess is not jealous. There is no sense that this approach to the spiritual has only one right path, or one set of divine truths. People may find her through love, therapy, music or art, as easily as in a church or temple.

Aspect 7: Structures for daily living

In goddess spirituality there is no split between 'high' and 'low' areas of life. Everyday bodily functions and activities around the home, such as cooking, are just as important and sacred as philosophizing in universities or praying in churches. Indeed, both the body and the home are often described as temples of the goddess. This 'natural' spirituality does not work on a hierarchical model of thinking, but on a rhythmic one.

It could be said that living life in touch with the goddess is living life in harmony with its natural rhythms, psychological as well as physical ones. People need to find out what their own particular rhythms are. For example, on a simple level, some people function better at night and others in the morning. It is what some Eastern religions call 'right living', which means knowing intuitively which action or behaviour is most appropriate in a particular situation.

If one is completely tuned in to the goddess, then ethics and morality, rules and structures are not really necessary. But for most of us this is still a long way off, so we need to have some natural laws to follow consciously, what the Romans called *Ius Naturale*, or the law of Aphrodite. More about that later.

Most of us also need structures and rituals for our daily and yearly lives. We tend to create them unconsciously for ourselves all the time, including such actions as putting the milk bottles out every night before we sleep. Again, individualized structures and rituals are often more appropriate than ones that simply conform with social norms. But these can sometimes have more meaning if we connect them with natural processes. For example, using the new moon as a time to make fresh starts or start new projects can be very satisfying.

This spiral model is probably one of the oldest in human history, at least that is a myth that I like to believe. It is based on the natural wisdom underlying the pre-patriarchal religions. Many books have been written on this topic and many new myths about this golden matriarchal past have been developed. To me it doesn't matter whether these myths are 'true' or not. They are, I believe, useful. And to make this model come alive in this chapter I focus on one of the most powerful images of Western culture and imagine how she might once have been understood and used in pre-patriarchal times, and how she might be used again by modern women and men. Her name is Aphrodite.

Figure 1. Rebirth of Aphrodite, 1988

Aphrodite

Aphrodite was the classical Greek name for the goddess of love. 'Reclaiming Aphrodite' is a useful metaphor for transforming the patriarchal imagery and stereotyping around love and sexuality into a more modern, useful mythology. It also implies that once she represented far more than the familiar Greek version and was claimed and distorted by the men in power. Reclaiming Aphrodite means returning to today's women and men a set of meanings and useful ideas around Aphrodite that may once have belonged to her. We can only guess. But several other writers have suggested that she was once much more than the vain seductress whose only purpose in life was to make love.

Robert Graves writes in *The Greek Myth:*

> Aphrodite (foam born) is the same wide-ruling goddess who rose from chaos and danced on the sea, and who was worshipped in Syria and Palestine as Ishtar or Ashtaroth . . .
>
> The later Hellenes belittled the Greek Goddess of the Mediterranean who had long been supreme at Corinth, Sparta, Thespiae and Athens, by placing her under male tutelage and regarding her solemn sex-orgies as adulterous indiscretions . . . As Goddess of Death-in-Life, Aphrodite earned many titles which seem inconsistent with her beauty and complaisance.

And Barbara Walker wrote in *The Encyclopaedia of Women's Myths and Secrets:*

> Often dismissed as a 'Greek goddess of love,' Aphrodite was really much more than that. Like Kali, she was a Virgin-Mother-Crone trinity. She was once indistinguishable from the Fates . . . she was said to be older than time. She governed the world by *Ius Naturale*, the natural law of the maternal clan.

Aspect 1: The Source

Let us see how Aphrodite manifests in our lives by making reference to the spiral model just described.

The Source

In her first aspect as the source of all being Aphrodite is the golden energy from which all creation comes. She is the one 'substance' from which we are all 'made'. She is the experience of melting into infinity that is both death and self-discovery. The word *golden* was frequently used in reference to Aphrodite — gold as in honey, sweetness, pure bliss. She is in fact pure love itself.

In my own search for Aphrodite I wandered through Greece and Turkey, through books and life experience. But eventually I knew that she was in and of my own body when I had a beautiful experience back home in London! I was in bed, half-asleep, when I felt as though I was going down in a lift, deep down into the past. Then, as I went deeper and deeper, I had a powerful sensation of the inside of my body beginning to melt into golden light. It spread from the inside outwards. It was an utterly blissful experience of love. And I knew then that this golden energy, which felt so fully alive, was the very stuff I too was made of and would return to when I died. I also knew that she, the great goddess, was in my body, in its being, not some image 'out there'. It was a fully physical feeling of utter inner beauty. For the Greeks 'golden' and 'beautiful' had the same meaning and were both applied most frequently to Aphrodite. Now I understood what they meant.

According to Paul Friedrich in *The Meaning of Aphrodite* the words golden honey, golden speech and golden semen are linguistically connected. They probably had philosophical and religious connections too. In some ancient cultures particular words were seen as 'causing' the creation of the world, perhaps through their sound vibrations. In the beginning was the word. Aphrodite is the source of language and culture. She represents the words that can cause so much passion, pain, understanding and misunderstanding. She may also be the first sounds, vibrations from which matter is created.

Semen was seen as the moisturizing principle of procreation, of fertilization, through which great energy is expressed. Aphrodite was supposed to have been born out of the severed genitals of Uranus, which had been thrown into the sea by his son, Cronus. (This is the Hesiod version of the story written in patriarchal times.) However, her name does mean foam-born. And her association with the sea, also a primal source of creation, probably goes back much further. The great water goddess of old Europe described by Marija Gimbutas in *Goddesses and Gods of Old Europe* was perhaps the forerunner of classical Greek Aphrodite. As water goddess she was the rain needed for fertilizing the earth, as well as the great sea mother of all. She was springs and rivers, wells and lakes in her many different guises. But always she was water as source, source of desire, source of life itself.

The dance of life

A good starting-point for exploring this aspect of Aphrodite is the Pelasgian creation myth, which describes symbolically the ancient pre-patriarchal religion of Greece. Creation myths usually embody far more profound religious and phil-osophical understandings than many anthropologists and scholars have realized. In this story Aphrodite is called Eurynome, and this version of the story is taken from Robert Graves.

> In the beginning, Eurynome, the Goddess of all things, rose naked from Chaos, but found nothing substantial for her feet to rest upon, and therefore divided the sea from the sky, dancing lonely upon its waves. She danced towards the south, and the wind set in motion behind her seemed something new and apart from which to begin a work of creation. Wheeling about she caught hold of this north

wind, rubbed it between her hands, and behold! the great serpent Orphion.

Eurynome danced to warm herself, wildly and more wildly until Orphion, grown lustful, coiled around those divine limbs and was moved to couple with her. Now the North wind, who is also called Boreas, fertilizes; which is why mares often turn their hind quarters to the wind and breed foals without aid of a stallion. So Eurynome was likewise got with child.

Next, she assumed the form of a dove, brooding on the waves and, in due process of time, laid the Universal Egg. At her bidding, Orphion coiled seven times about the egg, until it hatched and split in two. Out tumbled all things that exist, her children: sun, moon, planets, stars, the earth with its mountains and rivers, its trees, herbs and living creatures.

Eurynome and Orphion made their home upon Mount Olympus, where he vexed her by claiming to be the author of the Universe. Forthwith she bruised his head with her heel, kicked out his teeth, and banished him to the dark caves below the earth.

Next, the goddess created the seven planetary powers, setting a Titaness and a Titan over each. Theia and Hyperion for the Sun; Phoebe and Atlas for the Moon; Dione and Cruis for the planet Mars; Metis and Coeus for the planet Mercury; Themis and Eurymedon for the planet Jupiter; Tethys and Oceanus for Venus; Rhea and Cronus for the planet Saturn. But the first man was Pelasgus, ancestor of the Pelasgians; he sprang from the soil of Arcadia, followed by certain others, whom he taught to make huts and feed upon acorns, and sew pig-skin tunics such as poor folk still wear in Euboea and Phocis.

Eurynome (Aphrodite) is described here as the dance of life energies before form, the unseen interconnectedness of everything. It is her motion that creates the first forms, and in particular the serpent. This image with its sinuous body and wave-like movement can represent the primal form that

Figure 2.   Reclaiming the Serpent, 1986

energy takes as it swirls through space. Modern scientists have shown the primacy of wave motion in all matter and of curling, spiralling shapes in space and on earth. The serpent as created by the goddess is the first form of energy and perhaps needs to be reclaimed in a world where it represents only evil. The pre-patriarchal goddesses of Crete and Old Europe were always associated with snakes or serpents. Marija Gimbutas writes:

> The snake and its abstracted derivative, the spiral, are the dominant motifs of Old Europe, and their imaginative use in spiral form design throughout the Neolithic and Chalcolithic periods remain unsurpassed by any subsequent decorative style until the Minoan civilization, the sole inheritor of Old European lavishness . . . The mysterious dynamism of the snake, its extraordinary vitality and periodic rejuvenation must have provoked a powerful emotional response in the Neolithic agriculturists, and the snake was consequently mythologized, attributed with a power that can move the entire cosmos.'

Seen as an image of the primal form of matter, indeed it does 'move the cosmos'.

It is interesting to notice that, in this older myth, Aphrodite actively creates her own phallic energy through 'wild' dancing. This contrasts with the version that describes her as a passive product of an act of violence (castration) and of a male phallus. In the Pelasgian myth it is *her* sexual, sensual energy that starts the whole process, not that of a man. Indeed the consort that she creates does not even take human form.

The male boasting that led to Orphion's banishment to the underworld probably describes the takeover in Greece, as elsewhere, by patriarchy of earlier, goddess-orientated religions.

Division into natural material forms

In this part of the myth Aphrodite becomes a dove, a bird ever since associated with love and peace. She is probably a later version of the Old European bird goddess who is described by Marija Gimbutas and also associated with water and snakes. It is in this form that she lays the world egg, another theme common in many creation myths. The egg, like the snake, can be seen as a symbol of the power of love to create, to cause growth and to make changes. Within the security of the eggshell, transformation takes place and new life is created. This is not the passive kind of love so often associated with the female. The egg power within human females needs to be reclaimed and respected today. Yet in this myth, as often in life, it needs serpent power to break the shell and expose all that has been created to the outside world.

Through this third aspect of the goddess, love is made manifest in the world. It takes form. In the myth it involves the creation of the natural world. We can more easily feel connected with nature when we commune with the goddess at this level. We can even lose a sense of being separate egos and know that we are a part of it all. In her ancient being Aphrodite was all of nature. We can be worshipping or celebrating her when we sit on rocks watching the sea or feel an inner thrill at the beauty and power of the gnarled old tree. She is also the feeling that we have at these times, sometimes called the aesthetic sense.

Another way of contacting the goddess in this aspect is through our own bodies. When we respect and care for our bodies we are worshipping Aphrodite. When we fully accept and love our bodies *as they are*, fat or thin, we are worshipping the real Aphrodite, not the slim Venus figure that Western culture made its limited ideal of female beauty. When we fully exist in our bodies, feeling their tingling energies and blocks and tensions, we are worshipping Aphrodite. Intense physical pleasure, including orgasm, brings us into direct contact with Aphrodite; it is the main way that the universal energies of golden love express themselves through our bodies. Pleasure seen this way can be sacred. Goddess spirituality does not require the mortification of the flesh in the way that

Christianity, for example, does. For Aphrodite, the body, all bodies are beautiful. And natural, empowering body pleasure is sacred.

Archetypal Energies

Jean Bolen in *Goddesses in Everywoman* calls Aphrodite the alchemical goddess because the energies that she represented, even in patriarchal times, were profoundly transforming. She has changed the destiny of millions: the power of falling in love shakes people to the very ground of their being. She used to be associated with the Fates and can be seen as the process of life as it weaves in and out of good and bad times, teaching us lessons, giving us surprises. She is often unpredictable.

In the Pelasgian myth she creates all the seven planetary powers, which can be seen as the main seven archetypal energies: the Sun represents illumination, knowledge and focus; the Moon, emotions and changeability; Mercury, intuition and magic; Venus, human love and beauty; Mars, fierceness and assertiveness; Jupiter, creativity; and Saturn, earthy sensations, boundaries and limits. Each planet has a Titan pair ruling them to represent the balanced male/female expressions of those energies. Astrology is therefore another way to worship Aphrodite.

As religion changed to focus more on a supreme father god and the division of labour for the others, Aphrodite got split off into only one of her many aspects, and became the goddess of love we know of through Greek authors such as Homer and Hesiod.

But even in patriarchal Greece she had a lot of power. Remember that it was she who set off the events leading to the Trojan wars. Her power was generally behind the scenes and unseen, very different from the forceful power of Zeus. She could be described as representing the great unconscious world itself, all that lies beneath the surface of conscious daily life. With her we are moved by all the archetypal energies of the planets, albeit often without realizing it. Facing her and getting to know her helps bring these archetypal energy patterns into our conscious minds, which we can do through therapy, through thoughtful astrology, or through any other method that helps us understand ourselves better.

Socially constructed myths and images

Aphrodite provides us with an image that is very useful for women and men struggling with the complexities of modern gender roles. She was a strong, independent woman who followed her own desires and interests, yet she still liked men. For many women today, being fully independent and sexually alive has meant cutting off from men altogether. And some feminist writers, such as Andrea Dworkin, have argued that any sexual relationship between man and woman must be tainted with invasion and domination, at least if intercourse is undertaken. Aphrodite had many affairs, but always with men (gods and mortals) that she wanted. Unlike many of the others she was never raped. One does not get the impression that she was ever invaded or dominated either, although she sometimes lost her lovers. She was never controlled by a man. Even though she married Haephaestos (the god of smithcraft), he did not own her.

Perhaps most important for modern women, she did not need men to give her status. After all, she was already a goddess. This is very significant for many women who, despite having careers and money of their own, often still feel that they need a man or even marriage in order to have social status. We need to remember that we are all goddesses *in ourselves*. This is harder generally for women to realize than men. As a friend recently remarked to me, after reading Jean Bolen's other book, *Gods in Everyman,* 'Men already knew that they were gods, so it doesn't come as such a shock as thinking that *all* women are goddesses!' Our culture has made us feel that only the Marilyn Monroes of this world are goddesses. We badly need to reclaim the idea that we are all goddesses and that our bodies, our lives and our sexuality belong to us.

Aphrodite can give us the courage to see our lives as our own adventures, with scripts written by us, not by partners, parents or by the patriarchy in general. If we choose celibacy or lesbian relationships, that is our choice. If we choose traditional marriage arrangements, that too is our choice when we follow Aphrodite. Of course for many women economics makes such choices difficult, if not sometimes impossible, to make entirely freely and from the heart. But Aphrodite bids us to disregard social pressures and conventions, safe arrangements and security, to follow the inclinations of our hearts.

In patriarchy this degree of freedom scares lots of people because it implies doing unacceptable things like leaving children. Yet they forget the *Ius Naturale*, the law of Aphrodite that includes mother love as an extremely powerful force. In a society obsessed with love in the form of adult sexual relationships this is often forgotten. In fact, for many women who listen hard to their hearts, their love for their children is stronger and deeper than their love for their adult partners. There is a natural order to the heart and learning to trust it is what Aphrodite can teach us. Even as a patriarchal love goddess she had several children, including one called Harmonia, whom she had with Ares, the god of war, and another called Hermaphroditus, whom she had with Hermes. Both these children are symbols of the reconciliation of opposites, something that can only happen when we open our hearts and listen to the wisdom of nature.

Personal myths and stories

I have found Aphrodite an especially important image for those of us who are feminists and yet not at present lesbians. The term 'at present' is important because change and flexibility in our sexuality seems to me another important feature of 'following Aphrodite'. Her attitude to sex and the body are relevant to people of all sexual groupings. But for presently heterosexual feminist women the whole area of relations with men is fraught with conflict and contradiction.

Marriage as it generally is today is a patriarchal institution that was probably set up to keep women from the kind of Aphroditic freedom we are celebrating here. It is changing and men are changing, but often is seems too slowly for the conscious woman seeking self-fulfilment. Many feminists have negotiated much more equal marriages, others have chosen not to marry but to agree arrangements with live-in partners. Still others have chosen to live with other women, with groups or on their own, with or without children. Some choose celibacy and others enjoy sex with men (to the surprise of some other feminists).

It is particularly important for the future that male sexuality is not seen as 'bad' and inevitably oppressive. Although it often is problematic under patriarchy, this does not have to be seen as the individual man's fault. Because male sexuality has been rejected; it has twisted in on itself and turned into hatred towards women, violence and the search for inappropriate but, for them, less threatening forms of expression, such as 'dirty phone calls' and even sexual abuse of children. If adults in this society had a more natural and open attitude to both male and female sexuality, including deep respect for all people, I suspect there would be much less child abuse. In the ancient pre-patriarchal rites of Aphrodite, both the phallus and the vagina were worshipped. The heterosexual act was seen as sacred and analogous to all other acts of creation in nature and culture. It was *the* reconnection of opposites where humans could re-enact the great mysteries of the universe. Under patriarchy and its hierarchies it is rarely any longer a meeting of equally valued opposites, but a power game, in which the woman cannot win in the end, simply because she is already socially defined as essentially inferior.

On my own personal journey I searched for truth and freedom not only through books and various spiritual disciplines, but also through following my own sexual desires. This led me to unconventional relationships, often with men from very different backgrounds and cultures. I had lots of adventures, but after giving birth to my daughter did stay with her father, faithfully, for seven years. I didn't know then, in my twenties, that I was following the path of Aphrodite or that I had anything to do with her at all, especially as I was not conventionally beautiful or much of a seductress.

I finally discovered Aphrodite in Turkey in 1987 when actually on a pilgrimage to honour Artemis, whose image and energy had been particularly important to me since my separation. Artemis represented for me the completely independent woman who belonged to no man. She was also a huntress who went out into the world assertively, going for what she wanted. I needed her image to help me feel strong as I built up my career and asserted myself more in the world. I had felt rather timid in the very male-orientated world of work, and finding ancient images of assertive goddesses like Artemis was as useful to me as any number of assertiveness training courses. So in that summer I decided to make a pilgrimage to the ruined temple of Artemis at Ephesus in Turkey.

The whole city had for hundreds, if not thousands of years, been a centre of goddess worship and wisdom, probably corrupted by the time St Paul got there. But still it was seen as a powerful nerve centre for the old religion. Indeed Christianity took it over very early on and decided that the Virgin Mary had lived and died there in order to keep some female element in their new religion.

But while the old Roman city is amazingly well preserved, the temple to Artemis is little but a marsh with a few broken pillars where once stood one of the seven wonders of the world. The most beautiful temple ever built in the Graeco/Roman world was now just a wasteland. I felt deeply sad. And then I felt angry, enraged by what the patriarchal religions have done to the old goddess beliefs, and to women in general. I wandered through the stadium there where Paul had preached against Diana and remembered how he hated women. I felt defeated.

But the next day we sat in the dark cool of a little Turkish tourist office drinking apple tea and were persuaded to join a trip to Pammukele and Aphrodisias inland up in the hills.

It was a long drive. We stopped at a Nomad's restaurant in the mountains where the owner persuaded us to dance around the chairs in imitation of a wedding feast! We also partook of the hot springs at Pammukele, where blood-red water bubbles out of the earth, as if out of the great mother's vulva. Terrace after terrace of salty pools created by this water cascade dramatically down the hillside. Nearby the tombs and temples of Hieropolis feel like the end of the world, or perhaps its beginning.

Although this whole area felt very sacred and powerful, the place that affected me most was Aphrodisias, the city dedicated to Aphrodite, up there in the hills away from anywhere. It was stiflingly hot when we arrived. Excavations were still going on in the vast Greek amphitheatre. We stumbled along little winding paths covered with brambles, in and out of ruined temples, baths, houses. One bath still had water in it, deep green, stagnant but timeless. Here the Earth was sexual. Here was the place where rich, ancient Greeks and Romans came for pleasure. Pleasure oozed out of the ground. Here beauty was worshipped. Beauty was enjoyed. Lovemaking was sacred. I did not know then that the place was once sacred to Ishtar, the great Babylonian 'whore', the goddess whose power, lust, creativity and destructivity pre-dated Aphrodite. This predecessor of Aphrodite will be looked at again in Chapter 3; here in the mountains it was her energy that could still be felt.

The sculptures in the museum there were some of the finest examples of classical art I had seen, tucked away in this secret place. I came away feeling energized and knowing that it was time for me to rediscover Aphrodite/Ishtar. I needed her for my own creativity. In Aphrodisias she had inspired 'great art'; perhaps she could help me start painting again.

On returning to London, I did two things as a direct result of the trip. The first was to take a small statue of Artemis, with some women friends, to St Paul's Cathedral. At first the

Cathedral seemed impossibly male, with all the busts of generals and other male leaders. It was only after we contacted the powerful earth energy in the mid-point of the nave that we discovered an alcove with a statue of the Virgin Mary and some candles. Here we did our dedication and prayed for peace. At that moment the choir burst into the most beautiful song, whose vibrations touched us even if the words didn't. I did not know then that St Paul's was actually built over a Roman temple to Diana/Artemis!

The second thing I did was to start painting large, powerful, female figures that were struggling to emerge from the Earth. At the same time many of them seemed merged with that Earth. They were an expression of the feeling I had of sexuality merging with the Earth and with its waters. The paintings became more and more explicit as I felt increasingly comfortable with this idea and with my own body. But it was still some time before these ideas and feelings were expressed in my own sexual 'rites', which I shall describe in later chapters.

Everyday structures

The *Ius Naturale* was the natural law of Aphrodite rediscovered by J. J. Bachofen earlier this century and desribed in his book *Myth, Religion and Mother Right*. As a young lawyer he became fascinated by hints in Roman literature of earlier laws based on the ancient legal system of pre-patriarchal society. He describes it as:

> the Aphroditean law which permeates matter and causes it to be fertilized. It is Aphrodite who fills the two sexes with the urge for generation, who implants solicitude for the offspring, who forges the bond between mother and child and secures the freedom and equality of all the progeny. *All special privileges are odious to this goddess.* Hence the equal right of all to the sea, the seashore, the air and the 'commis omnium possessio' (common property) may be traced back to omnium possessio' (common property) may be traced back to the 'ius naturale'.

Figure 3.   Ius Naturale, 1985

This is a profoundly non-hierarchical kind of law, which would also fit well into a 'green manifesto'. With the demise of communism and bureaucratic socialism, perhaps such law can help us find new, more appropriate ways of thinking about human equality. We are all children of Aphrodite as Earth mother or nature. We are all made of the same substance, we all come from the same source. Yet how hard it is always to look others straight in the eye and feel equal to them, to know that they too are from the goddess. After thousands of years of patriarchy and the 'superior' male god, we usually tend to look up to people or down on them. We either listen submissively or dismiss completely what they have to say.

Equality does not mean sameness. At its least it involves genuine, deep respect for self and others, and at its best it means that people, whoever they are, have equal status and equal access to resources, which must include a radical change in society's economics and politics, as well as in its ways of thinking. However, while waiting for Utopia, there are lots of ways in which we can incorporate Aphrodite into our everyday life. It could be said that anything we do with love is celebrating her. The smallest act, like chopping tomatoes, can either be done with loving concentration, being fully present and marvelling at the beauty of the object and the act (all that juicy redness), or in anger and haste, with our minds on something else. I once fell in love with a man because of the way he chopped tomatoes!

We do not need special altars to her, as anywhere can be a place for her worship. But many women and men today are consciously or unconsciously building altars for her, on mantelpieces, dressing-tables, or in any special corner of the home. Often these include images of goddesses (not necessarily Greek Aphrodite), but also there are usually beautiful natural objects like stones, and candles for lighting at sacred times.

Celebrating Aphrodite for some may include dressing up and adorning ourselves, wearing jewellery and even make-up. We are not doing it just to 'attract men', but for our own pleasure and self-expression. It's the same with our homes. Finding our own personal style and aesthetic, our own way of enjoying and expressing beauty and pleasure, is following Aphrodite. She also leads us into exploring and expressing our own sexuality as fully and joyously as possible, while still being open to other aspects of her laws, such as equality and the protection of children.

Sexuality and spirituality seem to be intimately connected, and we will explore these connections in the next chapter when we come to redefine the imagery and meaning around Eros, Aphrodite's son.

2

Revisiting Eros

EXPLORING THE DIVINE EROTIC

It is Eros who will transform society
Deena Metzger

The erotic arises from our deepest instincts and is the guiding light
towards understanding self and the world.
Elinor Gadon, *The Once and Future Goddess*

Most people at some times in their lives feel that they want
or need sex. But what exactly do we mean by sex? It seems
that in modern patriarchal society sex usually means genital
contact with another adult or masturbation. It is based on the
idea of sex as a physical tension that needs reduction through
climax. Freud's whole theory is based on this model. What I
want to explore in this chapter is a much broader and more
spiritual view of sexuality and erotic energy.

The very word 'erotic' can feel threatening to many people,
especially women. Powerful sexual feelings are often so
intimately associated with being dominated, overpowered and
out of control that they are simply seen as too dangerous. The
fear of this energy is perhaps at least partly responsible not
only for the crisis in male/female and other sexual
relationships, but also for a lot of the rage, frustration and
sheer misery so many experience. We have lost the art of 'living
in ecstasy', of living erotically.

In order to relearn this art I believe that we need two major changes to our thinking and feeling about erotic energy. The first is to see it as divine rather than 'dirty'. The second is to release it from the limits of hierarchical power relationships, where one dominates another, that still characterize modern society.

The so-called sexual revolution of the 1960s did neither of these things. It resulted in only a limited kind of 'freedom' that was often especially damaging to women who were still seen as the inferior sex. And even today with women demanding control over and pleasure in their sex lives, most men still find it hard to handle. Even in gay and lesbian relationships there are often deeply imbedded patterns of domination and submission. Unequal power relations have been so eroticized that many people can only feel sexual when involved in either a dominator or a submissive role. The task today seems to be to *eroticize equality,* that word still resounding with images of drabness, sameness and committee meetings.

Erotic energy is stimulated by opposites, by 'otherness', and by tension. Yet in a society where otherness is almost always identified with inferiority or superiority, it is all channelled through hierarchies of power difference. For example, many women still say that they are only attracted to 'powerful' men: 'Power is the greatest aphrodisiac.' And for many men the desire to dominate, penetrate and overcome is charged with all their erotic energy. It gets focused on desire to possess or at the very least to *do something* to something or someone. The idea of sexuality as *being* is alien to our culture.

If, on the other hand, we can see erotic energy as the prime energy of the universe wherever there are opposites pulling and pushing, creating the tension that moves planets and atoms alike, it takes on a wider dimension. Gender opposites are not the only ones that create erotic tension. And this tension does not have to have its focus on 'objects' to be acted on. Simply feeling this energy in our bodies may be our most direct connection with the universe, nature, the life force or even what we call god or goddess. Eros *is* the spirit within matter. Eros is the eternal dance between opposites, all opposites, equally valued opposites. Equality does not mean sameness. Difference is exciting, difference is erotic, difference is life. Difference does not have to imply hierarchy and domination, superiority and inferiority, or trapping the life force in relationships with rigid sado-masochistic patterns.

The idea of equality often seems to fail because it isn't exciting, it doesn't tap into our primal energies, it tends to stay in the head. Socialist regimes have often seemed rather sexless, while the Nazis with their uniforms and sexual sadism apparently seemed exciting. If we are going to move in the direction of increasing equality in all aspects of society, it is vital that we do not split our heads from our sexuality. This will be easier if we enjoy being sexual not only in the bedroom but in being fully alive in our bodies, in being enthusiastic, which in Greek means being filled with god, in respecting the healing and divine qualities of erotic energy and in thinking about Eros as a god (or goddess — Era) who lives in our bodies, in nature and energizes everything. We need to see it as the spirit flowing *within* matter, rather than outside and above it. Yet this change requires no less than the seeing of all as sacred. That includes our bodies. Even what we call mere lust is sacred energy in its pure erotic form. After all, it is the same energy that heals, that creates art and that glorifies god in church when people sing their hearts out to Jesus, their faces often glowing with joy and their bodies swaying.

Let us see how some of the ancient myths and images of Eros the god can help us today in thinking more respectfully about erotic energy.

Eros the God

Plato described Eros as both the oldest and the youngest of the gods. The Orphics believed that he was the first of the gods born from the world egg, without whom nothing else could have been born. He was seen as the prime creative force of the universe, a role that we will explore later. But the more familiar story is that he was Aphrodite's son. He is very closely associated with her in Roman as well as Greek myths and art. The pair could be seen as a sentimentalized version of the pre-patriarchal images of the great goddess and her son/consort. He is a particular, focused aspect of her more universal energies. The arrows that he is supposed to shoot are indeed very focused and usually relate to a particular kind of love, a romantic falling in love, a love over which we have no control.

Eros was generally seen as young and irresponsible, showing no respect for 'age or station'. Graves notes that he was never thought responsible enough to be admitted to the ruling family of gods and goddesses on Mount Olympus. Already by the time of classical Greece, sexual passion, which he represented, was not taken very seriously, not respected, no longer connected to nature's energies, no longer worshipped. It was seen as disruptive to society, a nuisance.

One version sees him as Aphrodite's son with Hermes, which is interesting as Hermes seems to have started life as a phallic pillar, a 'herm', which had been worshipped as a form of the sexual life force for thousands of years. Eros too was worshipped at Thespiae as a phallic pillar. Hermes was later identified as the god of magic, healing and wisdom and the conductor of souls into the realms of death. Barbara Walker quotes Plato as describing Eros too as the one who gave strength to souls to ascend to heaven after death. She writes that Eros was a 'kind of saviour', before patriarchal religions began to replace the older worship of sexuality as a primary life force. In modern psychological terms we can see our sexuality as being a basic expression of who we most deeply are, the particular form that universal energies take in the individual body, personality and life, in short our soul.

Eros, like Hermes, is often associated with the serpent, also a symbol of eternal life as it sheds its skin yearly but continues to live. The serpent is associated with healing and the sexual energy or life force that has actual material benefit to health. The serpent was known in pre-patriarchal mythology as the consort of the goddess, yet created by her, as in the story of Eurynome described in Chapter 1.

The Hesiod version of Eros's story suggests that his mother is Eileithyia, whose name means 'coming to the help of women in childbirth', helping with that other dangerous passage of the soul from the 'otherworld' into human life. Eros is concerned with passages from one state of being into another. His energy gives us the power and courage to cross the boundaries that could be too daunting otherwise. Sexual passion has often been associated both with death, through losing the everyday sense of being a separate self, and with birth, through the experience of being a baby again, being reborn.

The idea of Eileithyia as Eros's mother reminds us that 'there is no love as strong as mother love'. It is the love that literally keeps us alive in our early days. This love is also in a profound sense erotic. The mother is interconnected with the baby physically, as well as emotionally. Her breasts need to be sucked just as the baby needs to suck them. For many women there is also enormous erotic, physical pleasure in breast-feeding, which can be quite orgasmic at times. This fact is rarely mentioned in baby books. In patriarchal society the only powerful passion is supposed to be for another, non-blood related, preferably opposite sexed adult. The power and primacy of the mother-child bond is played down, maybe even feared and envied by men who are often jealous of their partner's absorption in a new baby or even in their pregnancy. It takes away from what patriarchy insists is the only 'proper' place for erotic love, with the sexual partner.

The Orphic Creation Myth

Orphism was a popular mystery-religion in Greece and Italy in the early Christian era which had developed out of the earlier Dionysian mysteries. The power behind everything was believed to be the great mother, Black Mother Night, Persephone, queen of the underworld. This is Graves' telling of the myth:

Figure 4.   Rebirth of Eros, 1990

This goddess, of whom even Zeus stands in awe, was courted by the wind and laid a silver egg in the womb of darkness . . . Eros, whom some call Phanes, was hatched from this egg and set the Universe in motion. Eros was double-sexed and golden winged and, having four heads, sometimes roared like a bull or lion, sometimes hissed like a serpent or bleated like a ram.

Night lived in a cave with Eros, representing her three aspects of Night, Order and Justice, and mother Rhea sat in front of the cave, playing on a brazen drum and giving the oracles of the goddess. Graves continues:

Phanes created earth, sky, sun and moon, but the triple goddess ruled the universe, until her sceptre passed to Uranus.

The end of the myth is clearly a reference to the change-over to patriarchalism. So even here Eros is associated with this much earlier time when Rhea, which is a Cretan name meaning 'the flow', was the form given to the forces that rule the universe. She was the human, material manifestation of the erotic life force underlying everything. She was recognized as having three aspects, the virgin, the mother and the crone; the giver of life, and also the taker of life. She is similar to the Indian goddess Kali. She represents a time before the male father gods took over and separated all the functions of life. She was the first trinity, the three in one, thousands of years before the Christian trinity.

The cave mentioned in the story may refer to a time when caves were sacred sites to which people made pilgrimages and where they probably enacted rituals, with dancing, drumming, chanting and perhaps lovemaking too. The caves could also have represented entrances to the great mother's womb, places to which the dead returned to be eventually born again. The presence of the great goddess as life-and-death goddess may have been deeply felt in those places, so they would have been seen as her home. Entering a cave may also have been experienced as similar to sexual intercourse and a place of powerful erotic energy. So it was a natural home for Eros.

The image of Eros living in the cave with the triple goddess is a useful metaphor for the concept that erotic energy already lives within us and does not have to be brought in from the outside. This is especially important for women, who are often taught that it is only through the attentions of a man that their sexuality can be aroused, and then generally only if they are in love with him. The more familiar myth of a male Eros with his arrows helps to perpetuate the idea of the phallic intrusion required for erotic love to flow. If a woman realises that Eros is already inside her, in her womb, in her vagina, in every pore of her body, she can know that sense of fullness, completeness and wholeness that is her birthright. She need no longer believe the patriarchal myth of needing our 'holes', real and symbolic, filled up by men. Our 'caves' are already inhabited.

Men, too, often have a sense of emptiness without another person, usually a woman, to fill it up. It is likely that our bodily differences have some effect on how we experience this primal erotic energy, or its lack, in our lives; but it is also important to note that in the Orphic myth Eros is double-sexed, both male and female, not the purely male, phallic energy that is so often associated with erotic energy or even libido. At its source Eros has no gender; it is pure primal energy. As it takes on forms through human bodies, it changes into different kinds of energy according to the particular kinds of material bodies it passes through. Gender is only one factor differentiating one body from another: health, openness and hormonal balance are just some of the others that vary from body to body.

Jungian psychologists and others have described females as expressing Eros through receptivity, opening up, connecting, containing, and so on. This seems to be mainly because women have vaginas rather than penises and the act of sexual intercourse is seen as the metaphor for every other difference between the sexes. Male erotic energy in contrast is seen as thrusting, penetrating, or even attacking. It may be true for many people that in the act of sexual intercourse Eros does at times express itself differently for men and women. But the experiences of the energy as erotic tension, melting and ecstasy can be similar for men and women. The 'electricity' comes from the same primal source. Patriarchal society needs to overemphasize gender differences and the primacy of intercourse in which the male penetrates the female in order to preserve the myth of male superiority and his 'special' relationship to Eros in its form of phallic energy. Redefining Eros is vital for a more genuine equality between the sexes.

To restrict Eros to this one human act is a tragic limitation of this powerful and sacred energy. There needs today to be a valuing of the eroticism of everyday life, a sense of feeling 'turned on' all the time in different ways by different people, things and events. For Eros is the spirit within matter. The golden-winged Eros of the Orphic myth is a beautiful image for living ecstatically. When in love with a person, an idea or an object, it can indeed feel as though we are flying.

The Four Heads of Eros: A practical exploration

In the Orphic creation myth Eros is said to have the heads of a bull, a lion, a serpent and a ram. Graves saw these as symbolic of the four seasons: winter is associated with the serpent, new year with the bull, spring with the ram and summer with the lion. But they could also be seen as symbolic of the different kinds of energies into which the primal erotic divides.

Eros as the Serpent, 1

The serpent can be seen as the basic force — sometimes resting and sometimes active. It can be related to the Eastern concept of the kundalini, sexual energy lying coiled at the base of the spine that can be raised to the other energy centres of the body through meditation. When this is done, the whole body becomes infused with sexual aliveness, pure energy, and feels blissful.

But what often happens in contemporary society is that sexual energy is stimulated from the top downwards by the eyes and brain, for example by seeing 'attractive breasts' or 'good legs'. Bits of the body become objects for this energy to focus on; we call it desire or even lust. The energy does not pass through the heart or belly.

There are many techniques for consciously raising this energy. One way that I like is a Taoist method that involves consciously 'pushing' the energy up from the base of the spine, through energy points on the back, then over the head and back down the front, accumulating it as spiral energy in the lower abdomen. This belly area, rather than the head, is often seen in the East as our real centre.

A lot of people in our culture, especially men, seem to have their top half cut off from their bottom half. They can love with their heads and hearts, and they can desire with their genitals, but the two do not connect up in the middle. One man who taught me a lot about spiritual energy in the body told me that with his girlfriend he could sense himself switching between compassionate heart loving and sexual desire, but could not feel both at once. Another man told me that he had the same problem and thought that it was because there was so much unexplored pain in the solar plexus keeping the two halves apart. It was as if there was no room in that area for the energy to pass through. Perhaps the emotional pain lodged there has to be worked through before the energy can pass.

Women can have the same problem, but they are more likely to connect the two and 'fall in love' with men that they sleep with. This may be partly social conditioning, but it may also be that women whose solar plexuses are more open to emotions have easier connections between the lower and higher energy centres.

Eros as the Bull

If the sexual energy connects the womb area with the genitals, it can create a deeper kind of eroticism than pure lust. Many women love with their wombs as well as with their hearts; in fact, the womb can be seen as a second heart. Men can also work on their own 'womb' areas to enrich their bodily and spiritual experiences.

An image for this deep eroticism is the bull. It was seen as sacred in many of the ancient cultures, such as the Minoan, around 2000 BC, when both women *and* sexuality seem to have been more respected than today. The famous Minoan picture discovered in Crete of people dancing on a bull is a beautiful metaphor for celebrating the extremely powerful sexual energy that comes from the belly as well as from the genitals.

Graves also associates the bull with Dionysus and with the new year. It is so powerful that it can create death as well as new life: Dionysus was ritually torn to pieces each year and then reborn (see Chapter 7). Deep sexual ecstasy is often linked to death.

This bull energy is often seen as masculine and is perhaps the kind of energy lost by many of the 'new men' of today, who are living primarily in their heads and hearts. The 'wild man', however, lives on in the belly. But women have this energy too. In fact it is the kind of energy men are most frightened of: the term 'hysteria' comes from the Greek word for womb, and was coined because 'mad' women were said to be suffering from 'wandering of the womb'. And indeed, when this energy is not expressed or is distorted, it can feel like madness. Dionysus's maenads were wild women who danced and sang and got drunk with him on the mountain tops. It is akin to what has been called the 'red' energy of menstruating (and pre-menstruating) woman, who often feels a very active kind of sexuality at this time of the month. The roaring of the bull is the deep vibration of this energy charging passionately into adventures. If repressed it is likely to lead to a variety of problems, which for women are often associated with the womb, such as pre-menstrual tension.

Eros as the Ram

The next 'head' of Eros to be expressed is the bleating of the ram, associated with spring. The ram is also, like the bull, a sacrificial animal in many cultures. But it goes more passively to its death. It is perhaps the energy of the solar plexus, the pain of sacrificing for love, the pain of separation, the pain of too much tenderness, even the pain of knowing too much. This energy centre is often associated with knowledge and the intellect, intuition and wisdom.

The ram, as representing the constellation of Aries, is also the springtime initiator and the fire of passion. But this passion is a more knowing, less 'blind' kind of feeling. It is perhaps the longing to be with the beloved, the longing to seek them out, the longing to know them completely. It is also the place of empathy, of direct connection with another's soul. It is gentler than the bull energy, but when linked with the lower energy centres it can involve a magnificent joy that satisfies the hunger for love so many feel in their solar plexus area.

Eros as the Lion

Then we reach the heart and throat energy centres, which can be associated with the lion of summer. This is where the energy is experienced as compassion, as warmth and as caring feelings connected with the powerful lion. The protectiveness that the lioness feels towards her cubs is the perfect metaphor for this kind of strong loving. It is not a weak, sentimental kind of energy, but a powerful energy directed towards the world, driving people to act on behalf of others, to cross continents or face great dangers. The roaring of the lion is not to be ignored. It seems a far cry from the embarrassed gestures on Valentine's Day that pass for love in our culture. It isn't an energy just for a lover or even a child, it is energy that can be poured out endlessly towards other people, work, nature, ideas or even life itself. When it is empowered by the lower energy centres it can keep on flowing and more pours back in. It doesn't have to come from other people.

When this energy comes to the throat energy centre it finds expression in words, sounds and acts of creativity, as well as in direct physical expressions towards another such as kissing, hugging, smiling, laughing. Many cultures encourage the blocking of this energy centre, keeping it firmly controlled by the head above it. Bringing energy up from the lower centres through all the other centres, rather than just down from the head, makes expression so much stronger. Shouting and crying can help unblock it. For it often seems that energy gets distorted along the way; it gets turned into rage, perhaps in the belly, or into great pain, perhaps in the solar plexus, and needs to be let out before the purely erotic energy can come through.

Eros as the Serpent, 2

Finally we come to the higher energy centres, represented once again by the hissing serpent. Here in the third-eye area erotic energy can turn directly into ecstasy and the serpent can flow through the whole body. It is not necessary to be with or see another person and is often experienced in meditation. Sometimes it seems as though the erotic energy shoots straight up to this centre. It can overwhelm the person with an ecstasy that is hard to live with. Inability to sleep or even eat can be the result. Then it is important to channel it back so that it 'takes in' the other energy centres on the way.

The serpent moves in and out of everything and keeps moving and changing. It represents the life force, which is the same erotic energy, but not focused or trapped in only one part of the body. This is the golden light, the tingling energy of Aphrodite that can be felt all over the body, flowing through us. It is like electricity. The hissing of the serpent may be the primal sound vibration of all matter, infusing it with life.

Then, at the top of the head, this serpent energy links in with the energies of the universe outside the body. It may feel like a dissolution of the self into white or golden light, or it may take other forms. Here there can be the love that is merging with everything. The serpent needs to keep moving so that this energy (which is indeed the divine erotic at its most divine) can be brought into the body, back to base and cycled round all over again.

The serpent is probably the most ancient and universal symbol for erotic energy in its wider context. In goddess-orientated cultures it was often seen as her consort. Its movements seem to mimic the great flows of this 'electrical' energy in the earth, in our bodies, in the spiralling universe. Life does not move in straight lines. Rather it moves in rhythms, backwards as well as forwards. It wiggles. In patriarchy it has been seen as evil, precisely because of this connection with the primal powers of nature, the rhythms of life, earthy sexuality and deep ecology. This is even more frightening than the purely phallic symbolism that has more recently been associated with it. The serpent did not tempt Eve merely to have sexual intercourse, it tempted her to try to know the secrets of nature, the mysterious spirit that flows within her.

But how does all this relate to real-life relationships and everyday experience?

Loving with Eros/Era

The serpent energy has been trapped for thousands of years in the rigid, hierarchical boxes of patriarchal society. Eros has been imprisoned in the marriage institution or confined to the underworld of the artist, the unconscious and perhaps the pop concert. And always there have been tops and bottoms: the adored star, the beloved, and then below, the ones who adore, the fans. The beautiful and the ugly, the young and the old. (Only the young and beautiful are supposed to have sex.) To fully release erotic energy from its social imprisonment requires the difficult task of loosening up deeply imbedded hierarchical categories of thought. The pyramid form is not an appropriate one for Eros. Its form is one of rhythmic movement backwards and forwards, up and down. A rhythm model of thinking is a vital accompaniment to the release of Eros. What does this mean in practice?

A rhythmic way of thinking does not necessarily mean no structure at all and everyone just goes about 'having sex' all the time. It works on the principle of interrelated opposites. For example, in relationships people need times to let go *and* times to be in control, times to restrain, hold back, sacrifice *and* times to indulge. Life and relationships do not always have a one-directional goal. They don't always go on getting better and better or bigger and bigger. There are natural cycles to relationships. There can be purposes other than marriage or lifetime commitment. There is a rhythm between the opposites of freedom and commitment. Too much of one and we tend to need the opposite. Too much sex and we might need a time of celibacy. We also have different needs at different times in our lives.

Eroticizing equality is not only about breaking down sex and gender stereotyping; it is also about restructuring the very models that we use to think with. Many people are questioning gender-bound roles such as the dominant male and submissive female, but we also need to rethink the whole structure of superiority and inferiority in all our concepts. We need to let go of the idea that the mind should control the body and see them as equal partners in our rhythmic dance of life. To live comfortably with Eros we need new mental models, so that we can experience the energy and the love without immediately putting it in boxes that say, 'I feel sexy so I must make love to that man/woman'; 'I'm in love, so we must get married'; 'I only feel alive when I am with my beloved. They "cause me" to be alive.' We can recognize that the 'other' is in a sense only a stimulus to awaken our *own* loving, sexual energies.

Our choice of stimulus, or love object, is greatly affected by our social conditioning, the media and our modern mythologies of attractiveness. But the energy that we feel towards them, which is undoubtedly intensified if they feel the same, is from and within us, from the universe and the goddess. It is still there even if unreciprocated. I sometimes imagine the world as full of tingling love energy always available to us.

We talk about 'falling in love' with the implication that love is already there as a vast sea in which we may be immersed for a while. But the expression also implies that we have no control, as if we could not choose to swim in it. We must fall. Indeed choosing to swim in it by being in love with life and lots of different people carries a lot of risk. We can't blame anyone. We can't so easily use mind games or power plays around the one person on whom we have focused everything. The sea has tides and waves and rhythms that we have to learn to flow with. Falling into it accidentally is much easier. Choosing requires a deep understanding of oneself and others, and of the rhythms of nature. It requires working through or clearing out much of the childhood pain and unmet needs that tend to get transferred onto the beloved and distort and block the pure energies that are present.

As a psychotherapist much of my work is concerned with helping people understand how they project childhood fears, hopes and expectations onto present-day relationships. These, combined with our social conditioning, are the main obstacles to 'living with Eros'. There is a very common longing for a mummy or daddy in the sexual partner. This can work if each takes it in turn to 'parent' the other. It can even be quite healthy. One day one partner 'looks after' the other one and the next day they swap around. In most relationships, unfortunately, one person takes on the parenting role most or all of the time.

Other 'baby needs' are more subtle, like expecting the other person to 'read our minds' like mothers are supposed to. And there is often the desire to control the other person, either as we were controlled or as we wish we could have controlled. While all these patterns and more are familiar in all kinds of relationships, they are especially deeply structured into heterosexual relationships, where women are frequently turned into 'mothers' for men to please, appease and rebel against. And the gender hierarchics dictate that men are supposed to control women, however subtly.

Many women trying to explore their own sexuality over the past 20 years or so of the women's movement have kept apart from men, either as lesbians or celibates. It often seemed impossible to feel free with men. This is not just sexually free in terms of expressing physical needs, which women have increasingly done, but free of the power games and stereotyping. But men too can benefit from such inner explorations, for most of their sexual energy is focused on women (or gay men), even if only as images in pornographic magazines. We are all thinking that sex is to be found *out there*. For many women, afraid even to acknowledge their own sexual desires, men are the beasts, the ones who are sexual and rapacious. For many men, women are the temptresses without whom these embarrassing feelings and sensations would not arise.

So how exactly do we explore this 'inner eroticism'? We have already looked at actual bodily sensations when this divine energy passes through us as different forms of Eros. But we can also use myths and images of Eros. Through our imagination we can bring in and keep this energy within us. One of the best known myths about Eros is the story of Psyche and Eros, which has been analyzed psychologically by several writers, but I use it in a simplified version. I believe that the myths are there to be played with and used according to individual needs and interests. Each person will find their own way of reconnecting to Eros or to their own personal erotic energy. The methods and personal journeys that follow are not blueprints, but just examples.

Psyche and Eros

I see the myth of Psyche and Eros as a love story that is a metaphor for initiation into the mysteries of the goddess, specifically Isis. It is not about two people, but about the greatest love affair of all, between one's soul and one's erotic energy. Psyche means 'soul' in Latin.

Psyche is female and Eros male in the story, but they are both parts of all of us. Psyche is a beautiful princess worshipped by her people but unable to find a husband. Her patriarchal father is very concerned about this, so goes off to Delphi to find out what is wrong. The oracle there tells him that Aphrodite is very jealous of Psyche and so she is going to be married to Death. There is a hint in the background to the story that initiation can take place only outside the bounds of ordinary social relationships. And it is no coincidence that the whole process is overseen by Aphrodite, the goddess of love in all her aspects including the destructive one. In order to start the process of initiation Psyche has to submit to death symbolically. She has to be willing to 'die' to her old self, to lose her ego.

Psyche is made ready to marry Death out on a rock above the sea, dressed up in all her marriage finery. Aphrodite sends her son Eros to prick her with his arrow so that she will fall in love with Death. But instead he pricks himself and falls in love with her. So at the last minute she is rescued from Death and carried off to a blissful life with the god of love. This stage seems to represent the initial bliss of being in love, or ecstasy after letting go of the ego. But she is not allowed to look on his face. She has no conscious knowledge of what is happening, just as when first in love people tend to be unrealistic about the beloved.

She eventually gets curious, however, as her sisters make her suspicious. Perhaps he is actually an ugly old serpent? So in the night she lights a lamp to look at him and prepares to kill him if necessary. A drop of wax falls on him and he awakes. As she has now broken her side of the bargain he flies off and abandons her. This can be seen as the stage of knowledge when that first bliss is broken by coming down to reality, wanting to know fully that which is intrinsically mysterious, or it can imply a literal abandonment.

Psyche mourns for her lost lover by the banks of a river, perhaps symbolic of the stream of life that goes on regardless. Pan comes to her and suggests she prays to Aphrodite for help. Pan can be an image of the wild, instinctual side within us all, which often needs to be released to provide the impetus for an inner journey. His is an animal kind of sexuality very different from the 'romantic' bliss experienced in the first stage with Eros. Both are vital for this journey. She has to humble herself and ask for help, and it's to the very person that caused her problems that she must turn.

Aphrodite hears her prayers and promises to reunite Psyche with Eros if she will perform certain difficult tasks. These can all be seen as life tasks in a psychological or initiatory journey. The first is to sort a jumble of seeds into groups, to put order in her life. Sorting out one's files, tidying the home, or mentally sorting out priorities in life are examples of this stage. Next she has to get some of the golden fleece from the dangerous rams referred to in the myth of Jason and the Argonauts. The fleece represents power and she has to be very brave to collect it. The development of inner power outside of relationships is vital, especially for women, who so often give it away to partners and lovers. Next she has to fill a special vessel with water from the River Styx, which flows for ever round and round into the earth and back up again. An eagle helps her by flying high and swooping down with the goblet. It could represent getting a 'higher' perspective on things, but also being able to focus one tiny drop at a time. Getting help from others is an important part of the story. For example, the ants help her with the seeds. Help often comes from unexpected, not even initially valued sources. Again part of this message is to appreciate help and support from every-where, rather than expect it all to come from one person.

The final task is to descend into the underworld and get a

special perfume that bestows eternal youth, which is in a jewelled casket belonging to Persephone, queen of that dark realm. On her way there Psyche has to refuse to help three people. This may seem callous, but she, like all of us, needed to learn to say 'no' and be assertive before the final stage of initiation. She then descends into the underworld, facing her unconscious, her fears, perhaps death itself, only this time she has chosen her path in order to gain reconnection with her beloved. She gets the casket and returns to the overworld but cannot resist looking inside it, although she has been told not to. As she opens it the fumes pour out and overwhelm her. She falls into a deep and potentially fatal sleep. There is often a time of symbolic sleep, stuckness or limbo, just before a final breakthrough in therapy or life, a time of consolidation. On another level the desire for eternal youth, which has reached epidemic proportions in modern Western culture, maybe the last stumbling block to full integration of soul and Eros. In order to 'marry' Eros to the soul, it is necessary to let go of any links mentally between Eros and youth or Eros and stereotyped beauty. It also involves accepting death and the cycles of nature, including ageing, rather than trying to fight against them.

Yet at this point Eros comes again to the rescue. It is in the end his love for her that wakes her up and carries her off back to Olympus to be reunited for ever. If seen in terms of human relationships it could seem as though once again the male hero is rescuing the helpless woman. But in terms of a spiritual initiation it is the equivalent of the Christian idea of the love of god. God, Eros, or the erotic life force needs our souls to express itself through, as much as our souls need its energy to fulfill themselves. Without the soul the energy has no form and without the energy the soul has no joy.

Marrying the Divine Lover

One way of working with Eros is to image a divine lover (of either sex). This person may be a figure from actual dreams, what Jung would call an animus or anima figure (i.e. an opposite-sexed image), or from fantasy, recognizing that he or she is likely to include elements of social and media stereotyping. At some stage it may be possible to image this person in unconventional terms, even as physically 'ugly', and relate to the divine beauty behind the surface. Many fairy stories involved someone kissing a frog or an old 'hag', who then turns into a beautiful lover. There is a deeper truth about divine erotic energy embedded in these stories than might at first be apparent!

You could image this person coming to you on a beach, in the forest, or in your bedroom. I often imagine dancing with them. And then after dancing, making love or just being beside you, they begin to merge into your body until they are actually a part of you. This total merging with the beloved can happen only in imagination, although it is what we so often yearn for in ordinary human relationships, and is perhaps a longing to return to the womb.

It is possible to symbolically 'marry' one's own Eros. Sometimes this takes place in dreams when the person is ready. I had a dream when starting this book of a divine marriage in which we 'swooned' off together in the sky, clasped in a kind of diagonal embrace! It reminded me of a Chagal painting and later I saw this same picture in an alchemical book. It felt very powerful, although I still felt I had work to do on my internal 'marriage'. I wore a snake ring on my marriage finger to represent this commitment to Eros. (During the same period I met several women wearing rings of their own choosing for sacred reasons on this finger.) It seemed to me that I now knew that whatever human relationships I had, my *primary* relationship was to Eros, through the image of a divine partner/lover, or simply as golden energy. It is rather like the way that nuns can be married to Jesus, although in my case it did not exclude human relationships. In a way it has helped begin to free me from too strong a dependency on human men, and gives a measure of inner security in a world of fast-changing patterns of relating.

Figure 5.   Alchemical Wedding, 1990

This kind of marriage can also be actually enacted, either alone or with others, as a ritual, or undertaken using conscious visualization. One friend of mine 'married' a tree while attending a workshop in the open countryside. She said it gave her great confidence and actually improved her relationship with her boyfriend.

For me this 'marriage' was a vital stage on my personal journey to reunite with Eros, a journey that had begun with a literal journey two years earlier.

There are many myths and stories about heroes going on journeys, usually across the seas, and having adventures symbolic of inner psychological growth. But very few of these have a female as heroine. Today women are consciously or unconsciously going on journeys, travelling to distant places, having adventures and experiencing inner change as a result. Many are searching for an inner connection with Eros, finding it easier to explore and express their sexuality away from home. Even package holidays can be used for this purpose. Despite all the potential for exploitation in holiday romances, the myth may be a useful one in the context of exploring and opening up one's own erotic energy, with all its healing power and transformational possibilities.

I had an important experience of this kind at a crucial point in my own life. I had been celibate for several years, during which time I had related almost exclusively to women both in my work as a therapist and trainer and also socially. I had needed to get in touch with my inner female power and sexuality away from men. During this period I painted and sculpted many female, goddess images. At first they were like embryos being incubated ready for birth. Then they became bigger and more sexual, merging with and emerging from various swirling landscapes. Then at last I was ready to reconnect with men.

I had been spending time on a small island in the Mediterranean called Gozo, next to Malta. It has a temple to the goddess dating back to 3000 BC and the land still oozes with spiritual energy. Each tiny village has a massive, ornate

Figure 6.   Calypso, 1989

'cathedral' as its church and, despite the patriarchal nature of the Catholic religion, one can sense that the goddess has never completely left this island. It is supposed to be the island of Orygia, where lived the lovely goddess Calypso and where Odysseus was shipwrecked at the beginning of one of the most famous tales of voyage ever written, the Odyssey.

Calypso seems to have been a very independent goddess, who took Odysseus as her lover for seven years, and then let him go, even helping him to build a raft when it was time for him to return home. She did not depend on him, it was *her* sacred island, and she could let men come and go despite feeling great sadness at parting. She is one of the few female characters in the *Odyssey* who is powerful but not evil, sexual but not submissive. She is a very useful image for women today who still want to relate to men, but from a position of strength, centred in their own 'islands'.

It was a good place for me to start opening up to men again. What actually happened felt like an ancient, sacred, sexual initiation into the mysteries of the goddess. But first I had to be very centred in my own female body.

I had spent a week with a woman friend walking over the island, feeling great reverence for the place. We sat for hours in the temple shaped into the golden body of the goddess, stone chambers of her breasts, belly, womb. I felt as though the temple and my body were somehow merged and that it was my menstrual blood flowing into the libation bowl. Another day we climbed up to a more modern temple on a hill, and I left a phallic stone and two round ones covered with my menstrual blood on the altar there under the bright blue sky. As we were coming back through deserted lanes, saying how hungry we were, a cart laden with food suddenly appeared as if from nowhere. A gift from the goddess? Now I was really beginning to believe in her, or it, or something!

The next day we went to the beach on which Odysseus was supposed to have landed. It was overlooked by the beautiful cave surrounded by alder and cypress trees and hanging vines where Calypso was supposed to have lived. Not a hotel was in sight, only gardens of fruit and vegetables on the terraced hillsides. I met a young man there for whom I felt a sudden, unexpected desire. We connected several times on the beach before he suggested picking some beans for me from his family's garden. I went willingly, up towards the gaping cave where perhaps once Calypso had taken Odysseus. I thought of the man as the guardian of the sacred beach site, the goddess's consort, the bull. He even had actually one at home about to be slaughtered.

Although it was Easter, it felt very hot. We pushed through the undergrowth, with red flowers and red soil, until we finally came across a very old stone well, hidden in the grasses. From the moment he revealed this secret place to me I was completely under Calypso's spell. This well *was* my vagina and I *was* the earth. Her power drew us into each other with an urgency that came from somewhere very old, sacred, primeval. My personal erotic energy was streaming through me and connecting me with what felt like the whole universe.

This was my first initiation by a human Eros figure, but I felt it could only have happened to me *after* I had dedicated my body to the goddess and identified it consciously with the land. Now I knew that I was made of the same stuff as everything else. My 'inner waters' became the streams of life, flowing back into the earth, the sea, the sky. After this experience I felt, for the first time, that I could die quite happily.

I also began to trust the goddess more, and believed that she would teach me through life experiences, rather than through my going to a particular church or group. I would start looking at relationships with men differently. It would no longer be a question of asking myself, will this last? Or, is this a suitable mate? It meant that every relationship was going to be important for itself and its 'teaching'. Instead of trying mentally to judge situations and relationships in 'normal' social frameworks, I trusted my intuition. Success in relationships was no longer seen in terms of how long they lasted, but rather in terms of my own journey and

Figure 7.   Aphrodite, 1989

reconnection with both my inner Eros and the universal Eros. My criteria had changed. Short relationships were no longer seen as failures or embarrassing indiscretions. And the goddess was subsequently able to lead me only to those that had a sacred nature and help me avoid those that didn't. When the ultimate aim of heterosexual relationships is no longer biologically to reproduce (I already had one child), all the attitudes and needs associated with parenting, such as stability, are unnecessary. Sexual relationships can then have other purposes. And one of these is 'spiritual production', through using erotic energy wisely for healing and for helping to integrate the so-called 'masculine' and 'feminine' within each person.

Aphrodite and Eros have led me down many strange and difficult paths since then. Sometimes I complain to them. But basically I have no choice but to follow.

3

Inanna and Dumuzi

NEW MODELS OF RELATIONSHIP

Relationships between women and men are in crisis today. This is especially true of sexual relationships, but it seems to be the case in all kinds of relationships, fathers and daughters, mothers and sons, work relationships, and in gay as well as heterosexual partnerships. At the same time there is an increasing idealism about having equal, sharing relationships in which women and men are partners. Yet the ideal is so often far from the reality. Unfortunately the unconscious, with its images and myths from 5,000 years of patriarchy, is far more powerful than any intellectual beliefs about equality. Here again there is a need to change the myths before the social structures can change fundamentally. In this chapter we will explore some ancient myths that present very different relationships between women and men: the myths of Inanna and Dumuzi, Isis and Osiris, and Aphrodite and Adonis. The emphasis will be on the enormous variety of possible relationships, rather than on presenting any blueprints or suggesting that one kind is better than another, as happens today where the heterosexual, lifelong marriage is seen as superior to any other relationship.

We also need to transform our basic models of thinking about relationships from hierarchical, linear, goal-directed ones to rhythmic, fluid ones. The gender hierarchy itself is still deeply ingrained through unconscious images of an 'old man in the sky' representing god. Even for those of us who do not see god as a person, we were brought up on male images surrounding the concept. 'His' representatives on earth are still generally men. All this seeps into the unconscious mind at an early age and vindicates the belief that men are somehow superior to women. This belief, however much it is denied intellectually, underlies many of the problems between the sexes. The simple act of changing god's gender is a profoundly revolutionary act.

Personified forms of the goddess can also help us with relationship problems that stem from our culture's splitting of its divine images into madonna and whore, or pure spirit and dirty matter. Many ancient goddesses, like Aphrodite and her predecessors Ishtar/Inanna, were both mothers and very sexual. This is an almost unthinkable combination in patriarchal society, which is ultimately geared to male power over everything, especially its children. It is largely this imagery that is responsible for the problems most men have with their mothers, rather than some unchangeable biological fact, as so many psychoanalysts would have us believe.

Because mothers themselves have imbibed this split imagery they often 'push' little boys away from them at an early stage, afraid of any kind of sexual connection. They too have believed that sexuality is all about the adult male's 'desire for an object', which Freud talks about. There may even be some fear and revulsion at the tiny male body, which the child senses. Any sexual feelings or sensations from either side are quickly repressed. After all, mothers are not supposed to be sexual at all. There are no images in our culture of the sexual divine mother. Yet for small babies of either gender the mother's body is in fact one of the main early sources of sexual pleasure, through suckling the breast. It does not necessarily involve the same sorts of feelings as in adult male sexuality under patriarchy, which involve the desire to penetrate, possess, invade. The child may simply want to merge with the mother, go back to the womb, feel excited without having to *do* anything about it. But the mother often 'rejects' the boy physically. She believes it's for his own good. The result, however, is millions of grown men with an almost unbearable tension between their desire to merge with the sexual partner and the sheer terror both of rejection and of losing their identity in that longed-for merging.

Under patriarchy boys and men are not only supposed to be 'other' and 'separate' *all the time*, but they are also supposed to be superior. With a more rhythmic model of being we can recognize the need both to merge *and* be separate at *different times*. There need not be the permanent pressure to be always separate. Nor need there be the constant pressure to always be superior. The enormous power of mothers over babies, dimly remembered by all of us, contrasts with the inferior status of women outside the home. So men often have a terrible fear of and even revulsion at women's power, of the very place from which they came and must remain separate from it almost in order to exist at all. Women are constantly complaining that it is when men get closest to them that they start to 'run away', often at a frightening speed. This is not a natural, biological necessity but a direct result of patriarchal split imagery and an either/or way of thinking. Either you are totally merged and lose the self, or you are totally separate. Men tend to swing frantically between these poles rather than flowing consciously between them.

Because there are no strong images of the sexual as well as the caring mother, the frightening as well as the nurturing mother, all these conflicting fears, hopes, sexual feelings and longings are projected onto real, live, ordinary women, women struggling themselves to understand their individual complex identities. They often become little more than hooks for the male projections. We need to resurrect some of the old images (maybe reconstructed) of the sexual mother goddess to consciously hook our images onto, instead of real people. Just imagine what a sexualized image of the Virgin Mary could do for Catholics. And the Protestantss don't have even a single female image to connect with.

We have to go a long way back to find images of goddesses that are truly whole and incorporate all aspects of woman in the one being. Most of the written myths come from times when the patriarchy was already well established, such as classical Greece. But we can get hints as to how it might have been before, when the mother goddess was also highly sexed. For example, Demeter, who was the classical mother goddess in Greek myth, is described not only as goddess of the corn field, but also as initiator of brides and bridegrooms. She had no husband of her own but was clearly sexually active. She gave birth to Kore (Persephone) and Iacchus. We are told that she fell in love with Iasius at a wedding feast and, inflamed by the nectar that flowed like water at the party, the lovers slipped out of the house and lay together openly in a thrice-ploughed field. Robert Graves related this to the ancient sexual coupling of the high priestess with the king in public at the autumn sowing of corn seed to ensure a good harvest. Yet she is generally only remembered for her motherly love towards her daughter Persephone, a relationship we look at later.

Many of the ancient goddesses had sons who were also consorts, for example Cybele and Attis, Ishtar and Tammus. This concept may derive from the belief that everything must first have come from a woman, all of creation going back to an original female source. So she must have given birth herself to her own consort in order to be impregnated by him, in order to make more babies. Whatever the origin of this concept, it does not need to imply that, for people in societies that worshipped such pairs, actual incest was the norm. It can even be a useful image for today to help us re-evaluate female/male relationships.

Today the woman is generally seen as the consort to her man, taking his name in marriage for example. As the myths imply, it may once have been the other way round. As in many other situations where there has been an enormous imbalance in the past, it may be necessary to tip the scales in the opposite direction for a while before eventually evening things up. To some extent this is already happening with increasing examples of older women with younger men as lovers, husbands or partners. More and more women, especially in the third world, are now the heads of households with their men folk coming and going, rather on the periphery. Without proper resources this pattern is usually economically disastrous. But given a different system of distributing resources and a different set of myths, images and values, it is actually a viable alternative to the patriarchal nuclear family.

Perhaps surprisingly men too can benefit from myths of the goddess and consort. New images can help them heal relationships with their mothers, which tend to affect all other intimate relationships that men have.

Aphrodite and Adonis

One of the least-explored myths is that of Aphrodite and Adonis. Aphrodite actually gave life to Adonis but then hid him in a chest and gave it to Persephone, queen of the underworld, to look after. In a sense she abandoned him to the 'dark' mother. The split between the beautiful, loving mother and the dark, 'devouring' one is common in the unconscious of all children, girls and boys.

Persephone opened up the chest and took the child to her palace. When he grew up she fell in love with him, and took him as her lover. This all happens deep in the underworld of the unconscious and is symbolic of what can happen between a mother and her son. She wanted to keep him unconscious and perhaps even smother him with her love.

But when Aphrodite heard of this, she returned to claim him. She also wanted him as her lover. He was apparently a very beautiful and quite feminine young man, perhaps the type that would today be called a wimp. Yet he was desperately wanted by not only one, but two goddesses. This can be a hopeful story for the new men of today who have developed their 'feminine' side.

These two goddesses could represent the two sides of the

mother/lover, each side having both negative and positive
aspects. The dark mother nurtures but can also smother. The
sexual mother gives love, joy and creativity but can also
neglect and abandon. Men (and women) need to face and
eventually accept *both* sides. For women their mothers are
models, for men their main image of womanhood. A common
pattern for men at the start of relationships with women is to
relate to the Aphrodite side, and then later on, perhaps when
they marry or start to live together, they want the nurturing
mother who they deeply fear might smother them. Sometimes
they withdraw emotionally or sexually at this point, unable
to reconcile the two aspects of their own projected
mother/woman image.

But the myth does have its own solution. And once again
it involves a more rhythmic approach to the problem. In the
story the conflict between the two goddesses is resolved by
them agreeing to split the year into three. Adonis is to spend
one third of the year with Persephone, one third with
Aphrodite and, very importantly, one third on his own,
perhaps in the company of other men and/or having time to
be alone. This division could be seen as symbolic of three ways
of relating to women, which are all needed at different times
for men to have a sense of inner wholeness and for
relationships to work.

The goddesses could also be seen as the 'inner feminine' and
are as relevant to gay people as to heterosexual ones. With
Persephone there is the unconscious need for mothering and
nurturing which everyone brings to relationships. Perhaps the
main difference here between men and women is that men are
used to getting nurturing from a woman, and so expect it to
come from the partner if she is female, while women are less
likely to *expect* it from a male. With Aphrodite there is a need
for sexual love and creativity, a vital part of any relationship
which, if denied, may be looked for elsewhere. And finally for
everyone there is a need for time and space alone. We all need
all three aspects of relating, but at different times. At present
many people simply swing unconsciously from one to the

other. If we could learn to flow consciously between these states, relationships would be a lot healthier.

In the story, however, Aphrodite wants more than her fair share, as so often happens with relationships. At this point she could represent the mother or lover who invests too much libido (sexual energy) in the child or lover. And this eventually leads to the death of Adonis. Such attention can be extremely destructive, killing off the child's sense of self or driving the lover away or into another's arms.

But the death of Adonis in myth is connected with the ancient idea of the annual death and rebirth of the consort/king. Some people, like Graves, take this literally and believe that king/consorts were literally put to death after they had served their 'term' with the priestess. Other scholars query this theory. Even the story of Jesus dying on the cross can be seen as a part of this earlier tradition. There are, for example, many similarities between Jesus, Adonis and Attis, the consort of Cybele. But this death and rebirth can also be seen symbolically. It represents the recognition that in nature new life often appears only after the old is allowed to die. Nature works in cycles, not straight lines. There is birth, growth, peaking, then a cutting down till eventual death, and then a rebirth and the cycle starts all over again. Adonis was supposed to die and rise again, like all vegetation. But unlike the Christian myth in which a father god raises Jesus from the dead, it is Aphrodite who raises Adonis, and it is yearly, not only once and for all time.

I believe that we all need to go back (or forwards) to thinking about life and relationships in rhythmic, cyclical terms. For men this is especially difficult as they do not have such obvious bodily rhythms as menstruation. So men need to reconnect with the ancient vegetation gods and 'surrender' to the goddess as the rhythmic principle in nature. This is very hard for men to do, although the spiritual rewards for those who have been brave enough are enormous. For a man it may be easier to start with listening to and respecting his own bodily changes and messages from the whole range of feelings, sensitivity to seasonal or even moon changes, and, very importantly, the 'rising and falling' of his own penis. These are all part of the great rhythms of life. All stages of the cycles are equally important. This is a fundamentally different way of thinking from modern society's one-directional models. It values only the erect penis and the phallic thrusting of ambition, competition and aggression.

Isis and Osiris

Osiris was also a vegetation god. Isis was the great universal mother of ancient Egypt. Osiris was born from her and became her consort, but also her brother, which brings in a greater element of equality than there is in some of the other myths. He dies periodically and is brought back to life by Isis. In one myth she is supposed to have swallowed him — a powerful image of the devouring mother. But she then regurgitates him as the child Horus, or the phallic moon-god Menu, which means 'he who impregnates his mother'. Here again are echoes of incestuous desire, the Oedipus complex. But the story is resolved in a very different way from the Freudian solution of renouncing the mother and identifying with the father. Here Isis actually gives him and *values* his new-found phallic power, but insists on it being used with respect to her.

In some variations of the myth Osiris is killed by his jealous brother, Seth. His body is torn into 14 pieces and scattered all over the Nile delta. Isis mourns her dead lover and goes searching for the lost parts of his body. This could be symbolic of the way modern men, perhaps even more than women, have been split into many separate, unconnected parts. The head, for example, is often cut off from the heart. It could also represent the way many people have to 'fall apart' before transforming into a new stage of life.

It is important to note that in all these stories the goddess deeply loves the consort, even if she is partly responsible for his death. It is a love that can flow with the cycles and changes, not one that demands permanent union. She mourns the lover with deep sorrow when he is gone, allowing natural feelings of loss as part of the cycles of love. And in the end it is her love that restores him to life. Men need to trust that love of the goddess as they may not always have been able to trust the love of their mothers or lovers. Women too need to trust her, but for men, who often unconsciously blame her for their problems, even trusting the feminine principle of rhythm is difficult, let alone a goddess image. Most even have trouble trusting god, despite his male image; they have got to be 'in control' all the time. I have found that the idea of *trusting the process* is a useful one for many people, especially where humanized images feel inappropriate. Men also have difficulty trusting 'feminine intuition' in themselves and others. This kind of trusting is perhaps the most important of all, yet it is still despised under patriarchy.

Indeed Isis can be trusted, for she finds and puts together all the parts, except one — the penis. And this she makes for him with her own hands out of clay. She gives it to him and with that gesture brings him back to life, simultaneously getting him to invoke all her holy names as life giver *and* death giver. He then stands up fully alive and virile. They make love and, in some stories, conceive the child Horus.

This story could symbolize the importance of male sexuality being ultimately a gift from the goddess, nature or the life force, which needs to be brought to life through respect for her, and not, as today, in opposition to her. It requires a recognition of the sacredness of this energy and the need to use it wisely. Male sexual energy distorted and allowed to run riot without that respect can be extremely dangerous. We see this today in such diverse behaviours as football hooliganism and child abuse. What this story tells us is that the energy *is* godlike, but only when expressed in the context of respect for the goddess. This includes respect for our mothers and all women, but also respect for the cycles of nature, our bodies and the bodies of others.

A worshipful attitude to lovemaking is a vital step in the process of healing ourselves and the planet on which we live. For if we cannot 'worship' the bodies of our loved ones and ourselves, how can we 'worship' the earth and restore it to health? This does not mean putting the other person on a pedestal, as often happened to women in the past. It means focusing loving attention on all parts of the body. It means making love *with* another person rather than *to* them or *at* them, seeing them only as an object of desire. It requires a sense of equality, in valuing both bodies, perhaps even seeing them as temples of the goddess and god, not to be invaded or desecrated, only entered at the 'right' time in the 'right' way with the 'right' energies and rituals.

Finally, the child who is created by the lovemaking of Isis and Osiris, Horus or Menu, is described as a phallic moon-god. This image evokes for me a clear picture of what 'born again' mature male sexuality would be like after initiation by the goddess. He is very male, virile, sexual, but listens to the moon and to the other rhythms of life. He listens to his own and others' intuition and respects women. Perhaps most important of all, he feels comfortable in his own male body, and with his penis in whatever state, shape or size it comes. Women have been working for years on loving and celebrating their vaginas, and now men, who appear on the surface to be already far too obsessed with their penises, need to learn to deeply love and respect theirs.

One of the messages of this myth for actual mothers of sons is to value and celebrate their sons' sexuality and not be afraid of it, disgusted or repressive. For many this may mean looking at their own sexuality and feelings about their own bodies. And it is important to stress that these myths are not to encourage physical or even emotional incest. A mother's erotic energy focused too much on a boy (or girl) can have a variety of damaging effects. But the natural joy of mother and child sensually relating, even with some erotic tension, does not have to mean either incest or the mother feeling that she must push the boy away to avoid it. I believe that all of us, and

Figure 8.   Vegetation God, Greece, 1991

definitely children, know intuitively when a line has been crossed into abuse or incest. It follows that the mother needs to have a variety of outlets and expressions of her own erotic energy so that it doesn't all get focused on the child.

Inanna and Dumuzi

Inanna was the great queen goddess of ancient Sumer, around 1500 BC. The myth of Inanna's descent into the underworld has been beautifully analyzed in great psychological depth by Sylvia Brinton Perera in *Descent to the Goddess*. Here I want to focus on the relationship between Inanna and Dumuzi. It is important to note that she was not his mother. It is perhaps a later myth in which there was more equality than in the ones of mother goddess and son consort. But it was written before the time when the male gods had completely taken over. Inanna is, however, originally the more powerful one, being queen of heaven. She had many images, including the morning and evening star of Venus, goddess of the borderlands. She is indeed the foremother of Aphrodite. Ishtar was her Babylonian equivalent and the Hellenic City of Aphrodisias in modern Turkey was in fact built over a sanctuary to Ishtar. So there is clearly continuity between ancient Inanna and Aphrodite/Venus. Both goddesses were also concerned with love and sex. She is called the hierodule or sacred prostitute of the gods.

Ishtar was also called the great whore of Babylon. She said, 'a prostitute compassionate am I.' But the meaning of the word 'prostitute' was different in ancient times. Even in the time of patriarchal Babylon and in more recent Hindu cultures there was a strong link between the temple and the prostitute. In the Hindi temples they were called the devadasis and they were there to dispense the grace of the goddess. They gave out kindness, which combines mother love, comfort, mystical enlightenment and sex. It may even have been only through contact with such a woman that men come into contact with the goddess.

If we go back beyond written evidence to guess about more genuinely equal cultures, it may have been recognized that many women find it easier than most men to be directly in touch with the kind of spiritual and erotic energy that we have been looking at in previous chapters. There may even have been a more sophisticated understanding of the fact that this same energy is what people use when they are prophesying, giving oracles, intuitively analyzing problems and, perhaps most important of all, healing. It is interesting to note that in Hebrew the word *zonah* means both prostitute and prophetess.

The power of these women, whose sexuality was seen as deeply valuable, is hard to imagine today. As goddess temples were probably often also community centres that 'owned' all the land and distributed resources, they would have had considerable economic and political power too — a far cry from the sordid red-light districts of today. When patriarchal religions began to take over, a vital target was the temple prostitute/priestess, and with them the whole power of female sexuality. Their special relationship with the goddess (which many intuitive men have as well) may have been one of the greatest threats to male power. It wasn't only about women temptresses seducing men away from 'higher' purposes; it was the fact that *the very 'highest' purposes are themselves expressed most directly through 'feminine' sexual energy.*

It is possible that these temple priestess/prostitutes did not originally have intercourse with any man who came to get their services. Intercourse as the only function of sexuality may be a patriarchal idea. They could have used their sexual energy in many other ways, such as healing, prophecy and providing compassionate caring and advice, much as modern therapists do today. Given the amount of power they had it is likely that they chose which men (or women) they would actually have physical sexual relations with. Indeed, in the myth of Inanna and Dumuzi, she comes down to earth from heaven to search for a mate, wandering over the earth looking for the 'right man'. He does not choose her. There are many stories even in patriarchal Greece about powerful women choosing their lovers, for example Queen Omphale of Lydia and Heracles, whom she actually bought as a slave.

Once chosen, the 'marriage' or sexual union was given great sacred significance. Inanna had the great tree of life cut down to make the bed on which they would make love. And then she is very active in desiring and welcoming Dumuzi to her bed. She says to him, 'Come plough my vulva, man of my heart.' And she endlessly sings his praises, reversing the more familiar prime role of male desire that today fills our sweet-shops with pornography. We can imagine that, rather than feeling penetrated or invaded by his penis, she actively takes it in, enfolds it, welcomes it. Even the image of the 'active' male principle bringing to life the 'passive' earth is patriarchal, and may not be helpful today. The act of intercourse needs to be equalized with both active and passive aspects of both sexes. And it may be that the most important part of the event in ancient times was the energy that is created when two people equally desire each other *and* feel equally powerful. This energy can involve healing both partners, and can also spread to others present or absent. It can also help in harmonizing the so-called masculine and feminine energies not only of people, but even of the land and whole community.

Inanna clearly loves Dumuzi dearly, but when she makes her visit to the underworld, she leaves him in charge. Unfortunately he starts to take over and seems to forget about her — a familiar scenario! When she returns Inanna is full of rage and actually wants to kill him. He has to run for his life.

This image of the enraged goddess speaks to many women that I have worked with. They are often feeling not just rage towards a particular man, but rage towards the whole male world of their mothers and grandmothers and of all the generations of women that went before them. In one workshop we acted out this myth with a group of men and women who had been working together for over a year, but who still had many hidden antagonisms. The men all dressed up as Dumuzi, painting their faces and wearing scarves on their heads, trying to look frightening and pretending to have 'taken over' the room. The women were all Inanna and went to another room to talk about their feelings towards men. They organized a dance with drumming to herald their return from the underworld and then moved back into the first room. For what seemed like hours the women danced, stamped and shouted around the men, who were visibly terrified. Eventually they were exhausted and sat down to face the real men in front of them as equal human beings. Only then could an honest dialogue about real issues begin.

By hiding behind the mask of Inanna the women were more free to vent their really deep anger towards men for taking over. For most women I find that this 'rage stage' is necessary before it is possible even to begin trying to have more equal, honest relations. And for the men it also seemed a relief to feel fully and admit to their deep fear of women and female power.

After the discussion in which some people cried and some ended up hugging each other, we devised a dance in which both sexes could take part and celebrate their sexuality and their maleness or femaleness.

In the myth Dumuzi is in fact sent down to the underworld (i.e. killed) but only for half the year. It is in fact the 'solution' of alternation and cycles in the myth that has the most important message for women and men today. It is yet another example of the rhythm model. Dumuzi must give up his power for half the time and only then can he return and be reunited with Inanna. Interestingly, it is his sister who offers to go down in his place for the other half of the year. So there is great love between women and men in this story, as well as betrayal and rage.

Alternation is a useful way of dealing with any sort of power, used for example when organizations rotate the chair of their meetings so that no one is in charge all the time. But for men and women it is vital. Most men fear that giving up even some power to women means that they have lost it for ever, so they daren't. If it could be seen as alternating, such a loss may not be seen as so threatening. For example, in a heterosexual couple one week the woman could decide where

she wants them to go out and the next week it is the man's
turn. This is useful in any relationship. One day one person
can nurture the other and then roles can be swapped round.
Giving up power need not even be seen as a loss. It gives
people a chance to recharge, to be a child again, to be looked
after, something we all need from time to time.

This same model can represent other, more subtle
'opposites', such as the conscious and the unconscious
(underworld). We need times at night to dream when we must
visit the underworld in order to stay sane. People who don't
get 'dreaming sleep' very soon become mentally disturbed. We
also need to get to know the unconscious and visit it by choice
in therapy or art, as Inanna chose to go down into the
underworld. And for all of us there are times when we need
to feel in control as 'Queen' or 'King' and times when we need
to let go and even humble ourselves as Inanna did when she
descended to the underworld.

The rhythms of alternation can help heal the many splits in
people and society. This model acknowledges differences and
does not try to merge the two sides, such as male and female
or powerful and vulnerable, into one. The rhythm flows
between them, weaving the opposites into meaningful
patterns, not trying to lump them together. Both are valued,
but at different times. There is a time for togetherness and a
time to be apart. A time for joy and a time for sorrow and
mourning. There must be losses in life and these do need to
be mourned, as Inanna mourned Dumuzi when he was in the
underworld.

We have already noted that some scholars think that the
representatives of Inanna, the high priestesses, would have
literally had their lovers killed and chosen new ones. But even
if this didn't happen in quite such a brutal way, it is possible,
maybe even likely, that these were not lifelong partnerships
akin to modern marriages. Serial monogamy may be a better
description. And this is in fact the reality of many relationships
today, even if the ideal is still lifelong monogamy. When
women do not depend on men financially they are more free

to leave (without having to kill the man off) once the relationship doesn't seem to be working.

The model of finding a special lover/partner and staying with them for a few years or months, mourning when it ends but finding another one in time, can be a very useful one. Couples do not need to feel that the relationship has failed. The old goddess and consort relationships were once seen as the 'highest' kind, not as failures, and these were clearly cyclical. We could think in terms of all relationships having their 'natural cycles' that need to be lived out. It may be seven years, a lifetime or just three weeks. So long as the opposites of joyous celebration and mourning are allowed to be fully experienced, endings do not have to be seen as disasters. In this age of uncertainty the reality is that there are many kinds of relationships and many kinds of love, but while all are measured in terms of success against a monogamous, lifelong ideal, most are seen as disappointments or failures. The ensuing feelings of dissatisfaction lead people endlessly to consume all the products of the market-place that promise 'eternal love', from plastic surgery to diet Coke.

Some Different Kinds of Love

Below I outline seven of the many different kinds of love there are in relationships and some of the typical modern problems and possible 'solutions' that go with them. They all come out of the preceding myths, and most are illustrated by stories taken from the real-life experiences of people I know and have worked with.

Isis's Mothering Love

Mothering, caring love is usually focused on one or more 'special' people. It can involve wanting to protect or to nurture or even to serve the other. It connects with the child within the other. It wants to give to the other. Both men and women have this kind of love but women are more likely to get taken over by it. What starts as, for example, cooking an occasional meal for the man becomes a habit, and gradually the woman gives up her life to take care of him more and more.

Mary fell in love often and easily, but each time she found herself gradually losing her power and sense of self. It was fine at the beginning when they lived separately and when the man was still chasing her and being romantic. But when they moved in together, she found herself quickly getting into a mothering role. The men would start doing less and less for themselves and would dictate her interests more and more. She even began to listen only to the sort of music that they liked. She was not only looking after them but looking up to them as well. Somehow they were more important. They knew best. In every other area of life Mary was independent and strong, a college lecturer, a feminist, an intelligent woman. But when she was in love the feeling drove her to want to give all.

When she managed to extricate herself from a man she had lived with for three years and buy her own flat she felt great relief. There was a massive burst of energy and she was determined to stay celibate for a while. For nearly two years she focused all her energies on herself and her work, her women friends and on personal-growth workshops.

Then she met Mark at one of these workshops and of could feel herself falling in love again. She was terrified. He was a successful writer and highly intellectual. Mary found herself beginning to agree with most of what he said. She wanted to spend more and more time with him and couldn't bear a day to go by without being in contact. Finally he suggested that they live together. That weekend she went to a workshop on the goddess and explored ideas around different kinds of relationships and the importance of women keeping their power. She decided not to live with Mark but to keep the relationship on a part-time basis. She filled her time with other things, eventually seeing him only at weekends, which were usually very exciting.

This worked well for her for over a year. But in the end Mark decided that he wanted to have something more full time, perhaps be looked after, and he left her. Although Mary was heartbroken, she did by now feel much stronger. And now she knew that it was possible to be in love without giving all. In her next relationship she found a man who also wanted a more part-time set up, and who actually gave her as much, if not more mothering as she gave him. He usually cooked and often allowed her to be the 'little girl' that hadn't had much chance of expression since her actual childhood.

Ishtar's Compassionate Love

Compassionate love can be poured out towards anyone. It is a focusing of all the heart energies on a person, regardless of what they do or look like. It accepts. It does not judge. In that sense it is a promiscuous love. It is not reserved for one special person.

Jane felt she had an abundance of love inside her that she wanted to share after a particularly powerful experience of 'enlightenment' she had one day while meditating on a beach. When she went back home into her ordinary, everyday life she found herself hugging everyone and being very loving to all kinds of people. But her boyfriend began to get jealous, and many of the men that she poured this love out to misunderstood her and thought that she was giving them a 'come on'. At the time she was in training to be a therapist, so she was able to explore these problems with her tutor, who was involved in goddess spirituality. She told Jane that it is this very kind of love that is the most important ingredient in good therapy, and that in a sense the therapist can be 'in love' with each client for the duration of the session. Ishtar/Aphrodite, goddess of love, is indeed transformational and the patron 'saint' of therapy. They also discussed the problems of male responses to female affection and the limits of living under patriarchy. As Jane progressed further in her therapy and took on clients and ran groups, she was able to channel her compassionate love energy in a productive (and lucrative) way.

Isis and Osiris's Sisterly/Brotherly Love

As well as being mother and son, and goddess and consort, at times this pair are also sister and brother. In Egypt marriage of the Pharaohs between brother and sister was common. This is the kind of love that comes with friendship and companionship, the sharing, warmth and familiarity of being together that keeps many a relationship alive after the romantic, in-love phase has passed. It is also the love of platonic relationships between people of the same or opposite sex.

John had a very good platonic relationship with Sue, which had lasted for several years. They had been at college together and were both active in politics. But when John got married his wife did not want him to see Sue any more. He could not convince her that it was a platonic relationship with no threat to their marriage. John had always preferred to have women friends and found this new situation rather trapping. Eventually he decided to leave and to live in a commune with two other women and a man. His friendship with Sue continued and they became lovers, but decided not to live together or to make definite promises or commitments. She didn't want children and was happy to take the relationship day by day. After six years they are still together.

Inanna and Dumuzi's Erotic Love

Erotic attraction can be seen as a very physical, magnetic pull between two people. Probably one of the most powerful forces in human relations, it can sweep away all the other forms of love if not handled carefully.

When Julie and Pete first met at a party there was an instant attraction. But Julie was very wary at first, as she was already in a very important, loving relationship with a woman. She did not want to endanger that connection but was fascinated by Pete, who seemed very understanding about her feminist belief that sexual relations between men and women are too deeply fraught with patriarchal power issues to be really equal. So they decided to use this very strong energy between them to explore how to have a sexual relationship as two equally powerful, highly-sexed beings. Julie told Pete that she did not want to have intercourse with him, but almost anything else would be fine. She also felt, as they spent time together, that it was vital that this energy should be dedicated to the goddess, who is most easily channelled through a woman. The goddess would let them know what felt right, what would be healing and what would preserve equality.

They met every two weeks for a year and spent hours meditating and sharing the sexual energy they generated. Sometimes they would go to sacred sites at night or when no one else was around, and tune their energies in to those already present in the place. Both were healed physically and mentally by the relationship. It also helped them to get rid of all the stereotypes and expectations of male/female relating, as it was quite outside of 'normal' relationships.

Aphrodite's Jealous Love

Possessive love, which involves wanting to keep one's lover to oneself, is a very powerful force, and attempts to deny or ignore such feelings often leads to unnecessary pain. It has sometimes been fashionable among liberal-minded people to argue that jealousy is wrong and that no human being possesses another. In one sense that is true. No one person should 'own' another, although patriarchal marriage is based on this idea. But most small children want their mother all to themselves and are jealous of others that she loves. And intense, sexual love does have a bonding aspect that is, in a sense, broken by being shared with someone else. Jealousy is hard to lose completely; even the most emotionally secure people may feel it in some circumstances. So people have to find ways of dealing with it or minimizing the circumstances in which it might arise.

Robin was very left wing and believed in open relationships with women. But when he met Sara he felt a very strong erotic attraction, more than he had felt before. It shocked him because she didn't have much in common with him and was not the sort of woman that he usually went out with. He told her about his belief in open relationships and to his relief she seemed quite enthusiastic. She would tell him about her other lovers, sometimes in detail. He found himself experiencing increasingly obsessive feelings of jealousy until he could hardly think about anything else. Eventually he realized that he couldn't bear it any longer, so he simply asked her not to tell him any more. What she did when not with him was her business, but he couldn't handle hearing about it.

Isis's Sacrificial Love

In many of the early stories of goddess and son/consort, the son is sacrificed, mourned and then brought back to life by the 'mother'. The kind of love that Christians talk about when Jesus died for our 'sins' involves this lack of concern for the self, caring more about the other and making some kind of sacrifice. At one level it can be seen as the literal love of a mother for her son when she lets him go, grow up, leave her in order to be a man. But in couple relationships there can also be this sort of love. For example, where a relationship has become too similar to a mother/child connection the 'mother' may need to say 'no' to the boy within the man, or the 'girl' within the woman. She may have to leave him or let him go in order for him to be more fully himself. This can be a necessary part of growth in any relationship. There may then be a time of mourning, as in the old goddess/consort tales, possibly followed by a time of getting to know each other better as complex adults made up of many parts, as when Isis searched for and found all the different bits of Osiris's body. There may then be a reunion as two mature lovers.

Ann and James had been living together for three years. He was 23 and the relationship with Ann was his first serious one, while Ann was 36 and had been married before meeting James. He had become more and more dependent on her and more and more resentful and depressed. So they decided that he needed to move out and travel around the world a bit. The separation was painful for both of them. But James soon found a new independence and freedom while travelling in Greece and Italy. When he came back he found a place of his own and had lots of girlfriends. Ann still missed him and went looking for him. They finally met up again and for a while were just friends getting to know each other better. Then after about a year they became lovers again on a very different basis, with separate homes and lives, but with a deep, mature connection.

Isis and Osiris's Spiritual Love

As we have seen in the two previous chapters, spiritual love is ultimately our own personal relationship to the divine energy of Eros that permeates the entire universe. But there are ways of working with, sharing and enhancing these connections in the context of sexual relationships.

It may often be easier to follow a spiritual path alone, even in a secluded monastery, than to pursue it in the context of human relationships. But the process of growth can be intensified and broadened to include the psychological as well as the spiritual in relationships with another. This is the basis of the guru–disciple relationship, and also of modern therapy, in which it is recognized that if the client is a little 'in love' with his or her therapist, then more emotional energy is brought into the sessions and deep change can happen faster. This is part of the process of 'transference' between the client and therapist, in which the client has powerful feelings of love, anger or hate towards the therapist which are similar to feelings from the client's past towards parents and others. The presence of erotic energy (through transference) does help speed up the process. Complete honesty and openness to another also helps to clear the blockages to feeling any kind of love, including the spiritual. Sharing the unacceptable as well as the acceptable aspects of oneself is a way of shedding the ego, a vital part of any spiritual path.

In a couple relationship this sharing can be completely equal, unlike in therapy or a teaching relationship. Both people also have to face the awesome and often frightening power of the other's deepest emotions in full flood. Men especially find this difficult, often because they cannot face their own deep feelings. It is like facing the goddess and the god in all their 'good' and 'bad' aspects.

Seeing the divine in the other is a vital part of spiritual love but, because our patriarchal society divides the divine into god and devil, virgin and whore, such 'worship' of the other tends to strip them of their full complex humanity and turn them into media images that are cardboard and one-sided. For hundreds of years, especially since the Troubadours of the Middle Ages (wandering minstrels who sang love songs to the ladies of the court), women have been put on pedestals and worshipped from afar as 'goddesses', but not as full human beings. This kind of superficial worship can, of course, happen towards men as well. In fact it is the essence of what is generally called romantic love. The other person is turned into an image of god or goddess and loved for that reason. They may even be seen as perfect. In goddess spirituality the full human being, warts and all, is seen as itself divine. The person, all people, can be seen as temples or channels of the divine energy. And this may be especially clear when the person is sexually aroused. In patriarchal society men often worship the *image* of a woman quite regardless of her inner state or actual feelings or conscious connection to the divine. She is rarely encouraged to allow herself to feel, let alone express, her own inner sexuality as opposed to putting on a show for the man.

In equal sacred sexuality there isn't even any need to put an image on the other at all. Both partners simply are in the presence of, and indeed are themselves both goddess and god, genderless divinity. It does not involve looking up to the other, as in patriarchal worship. There is just a trance-like awareness of both bodies as divine. (Of course, all this applies to gay and lesbian relationships as well as heterosexual ones.)

We can see the other as he or she really is. So often, especially in youthful love, we fall in love with someone who represents our own inner 'opposite-sexed' side, what Jung called the animus in woman and the anima in man. Or we see in them our mothers and fathers, siblings, or stereotyped images. In equal sacred sexuality it helps if both partners have taken back these projections as far as possible and, as it were, 'married' their inner partner/lover, as described in Chapter 2. They will then be clearer about relating on the level of basic energies, without mental distortions. Images may still come up spontaneously, but these are more likely to be divine images that are appropriate to the energies present, such as Inanna for the actively receiving female. Divine images evoked in trance-like love can be used by both men and women. They will arise from the soul, not the head.

Many people throughout the ages have found that one of the quickest ways to reach a trance state or feel mystical connection with the universe is through being in a sexual and loving situation not aimed solely at orgasmic release. But unlike most Eastern methods, such as Tantra, which involve a focus on techniques and practices and tend to emphasize 'keeping in' the energy by not ejaculating, in goddess spirituality all that is required is to let the energy itself take over. People may need to feel their own divine energy first, through meditation or simply through being fully present in their sexually alive, turned-on bodies. They may need to feel in love, in the moment at least, and for some these states are reached only occasionally in the early stages of a relationship. But it is possible to cultivate the feeling of being in love, within the present moment, as a gift of divine energy that is not at the mercy of whatever else is, or is not, going on in the relationship.

It may help to start with prolonged eye contact and it may be important to keep this up throughout, especially if one or other keeps going off into stereotyped gender responses or game playing. The enormous amount of energy that can be generated gives far greater ecstasy than all the mental games and stereotypes that so often form the basis of sexual relations. In fact at this stage these can be allowed to come up and be laughed at, played with, and then discarded. There is no need to role play or dress up, but this too may come up naturally and be played with and let go. Ultimately the goddess is in control, neither partner is. Men who are used to being in control may find this especially threatening, and as 'her' energy is most quickly channelled through a female body it might mean the woman appearing to be more in charge.

Sacred sexuality is not about holding back orgasms for the sake of keeping in the power, as is suggested, usually for men's benefit, in many of the Eastern techniques. It is about going with the flow of the energy within and between the two, letting go totally of the ego. It involves an intense loving and living in the eternal present, regardless of goals either of love-making or of the relationship. While many people may only be able to feel such heightened 'in love' feelings within a long-term, committed relationship, others may be able to access such feelings in other situations, which may not even be romantic in the stereotyped meaning of the word. Sacred sex is not about desire for an object, or the need for personal, physical satisfaction. Both people need to be wholly present in themselves and in awareness and love of the other whole person, body and soul. It is a way of bringing the soul into direct alignment with the body. It is in fact bringing spirit into matter.

It may also involve a harmonizing of the so-called masculine and feminine energies. (I dislike both terms as they are so over-burdened with socio-cultural meanings. But, as I have suggested before, differently made bodies do probably channel

Figure 9.   Rising Sap, 1991

even the same energies differently.) Both men and women have passive *and* active modes of love-making that can interact with each other in a large variety of permutations and be endlessly creatively explored, once stereotyping is let go of. The two bodies can even be experienced as expressions of fundamental forces of the universe, from one opposite to another, in a dance of love. In that sense we can all be both goddess and god, both the source of all joy and creativity, and the active round of birth, growth, peak, decay to death and rebirth — of, for example, the erection, the energy, the excitement. Both can identify with the earth, and both can die back into her. There can be both merging and emerging, both entering and leaving, unifying and separating, receiving and giving, holding back and letting go, advancing and retreating. Actual intercourse may not even be necessary.

I have concentrated on the physical, sexual aspects of spiritual love because this is less understood in modern Western society than other kinds, such as the spiritual tie that conventional marriage is supposed to bestow. There are undoubtedly other kinds of spiritual connections between people, some of which do not require physical contact at all. But the relationship between Isis and Osiris was very physical, and directly connected to the land and the seasons. He was the flooding and receding River Nile, she was the land. She was the ground of being, the throne on which all else sits, and he was the eternal round of nature. Through their love for each other, their separations and searches and finally their mating, the opposites of nature were harmonized. If more couples today can have even an inkling of what love-making with that connection may be like, great healing can take place, not just between woman and man, man and man, woman and woman, but of the planet itself.

4

Helen of Britain

LOVING THE LAND, LOVING OUR BODIES

One of the deepest loves that many people have is their love of place, of land, the land of home, sacred land, land imbued with special memories. This kind of love is usually far more powerful and emotional than the more abstract love of the whole planet; yet this love of all the Earth, this more universal connection with nature, is vital for our very survival. It is a very important task to transform our love of particular pieces of earth into a love of the whole Earth, although it may need to be through our own particular connections to it in everyday life. This has to be far deeper than living a life that is ecologically sound, important though that is; our unconscious psyche must be involved. Myths and images that help us in this transformation are needed to provide alternatives to the myths and images that bind people to their 'homelands' or to the artificial boundaries used to create nation states.

Still today, many, if not most, of the conflicts and wars of the world are connected with feelings of possessive love towards particular pieces of this planet. It may be love of a 'homeland' from which a people's ancestors came, that now has some other group of people living in it. For many, their whole identity still rests on identification with specific bits of land. As communism has disintegrated in the Eastern bloc, nationalism, often connected to land, has come pouring back, with a passion some thought had long ago disappeared. This 'love' of land, and the group identities associated with it, goes far deeper than the surface ideologies of communism or even of green politics and beliefs in internationalism. It goes back a very, very long way to thousands of years ago, when humans first began to see land as possession, as status, as owned by a group or individual. It goes back to the dawn of patriarchy when the principle of total control *over* nature took over from the principle of co-operation *with* her, when hierarchical, dominator cultures took over from partnership, rhythmic ones. But this possessiveness is not an essential feature of human nature: anthropology shows us a very wide range of human societies with an equally wide range of relationships to nature and to land.

I believe that a deep transformation of our modern relationship to nature and land is essential, but cannot be achieved by reason alone. We can be provided with endless facts and figures about, for example, the cutting down of the rainforests. But this is not enough. A tiny minority of activists will feel strongly about such distant events and may even manage to whip up powerful emotions in others, for a few days. This may even help to change the policies of the World Bank, for example, which is vital, but it is not enough. Some might say that we need a 'green religion' for the change to go deep enough, and small groups of people are indeed talking about eco-spirituality, creation spirituality, and so on. But we need even more fundamental a change than that. For if we are going to have a really deep, loving connection to the Earth, not just when in church or at meetings, we need to relate differently to that aspect of nature or part of the Earth that we are with in the here and now, wherever we are. Even if we are living in the city we can feel the land and the water deep beneath the city pavements. Our homes can be temples all the time, not just when we light candles. And, perhaps most important of all, our bodies are the piece of nature that we always have with us. These too can be permanent temples.

It seems to me that there are two levels on which we can develop this love of the Earth. The first is the love of the present place: our bodies and whatever land they happen to be on at the moment. Wherever a person is living, there are likely to be sites nearby that can be felt as especially sacred. A park, a tree or a river can feel just as sacred as sitting in the church of one's home town. As I live in London I am especially interested in finding sacred connections to nature in the city, and part of this chapter is devoted to this topic and the mythology that has helped me and many others.

The second level is that of the whole planet, popularizing and deepening the love that many are beginning to feel for this blue–green ball that is our shared home. Use of the name Gaia, the Greek name for the Earth goddess, has helped to make us feel that she is alive as a whole. She is a being, and she has her own self-regulating processes that keep her balanced. She tends to be imaged more easily as a mother goddess than as male. Perhaps for some she could embody all those powerful longings that we have for a kind of all-encompassing great mother. Although we have a long way to go before this feeling is as strong and as profoundly internalized in our hearts and minds as the male supergod still is, there are signs of hope.

As representatives of the planet Earth (like statues representing the gods), bits of nature close at hand, like plants, stones and our own bodies, can 'stand in' for her. They can be local expressions of her wider wisdom. They do not need to be seen as objects of possession in themselves. Land can also be looked at in this way, rather than as a thing to be owned.

These two levels could be seen as opposite but interconnected aspects of the whole. They can be compared to increased centralization and world unity on the one hand and decentralization and devolution of power on the other. These two processes are often seen as incompatible in patriarchal either/or terms. But perhaps they are *both* the way forward for our plant. What they both leave out as no longer useful is the middle level, the nation state with its artificial boundaries. Instead of identity and allegiance being to one's nation, there is *both* the sense of common humanity and allegiance to the planet *and* the local, specific identity of the place where you happen to be and the people you happen to be with. They may be chosen not for reasons of having common ancestors or racial origins, but for such factors as shared interests, shared neighbourhoods and shared personal love.

But this way of being cannot work within the old patriarchal and hierarchical frameworks in which people, groups and lands are divided into superior and inferior. For in order to feel a sense of common humanity there is a need to see the other as different but equal, not above or below oneself. Once more we are back to the idea of a rhythm model in which difference is respected and celebrated and not turned into a hierarchy. Today, many people's self-esteem and very identity depends on them seeing some other person as inferior or some other place as 'lower'.

In a rhythmic system people would have a whole range of identities open to them, some of which might relate to their racial or cultural origins, and others of which would not . They would not have to feel stuck in just one identity in order to feel good. Nor will one identity be seen as superior to another. For every human body is a representative of the Earth goddess, of the life force, of nature herself. Loving oneself and one's own body and the whole of nature can take the place of loving only one's family, clan, or friends from identical backgrounds. It can also replace loving only one piece of land and not the rest. Nationalism and racism are simply no longer useful.

One of the dangers of the modern uprising of interest in the pagan roots of British culture, especially in the Celtic tradition, is that it could be used to fuel a new round of nationalism and racism. Such images as the Holy Grail were, after all, used by the Nazis to fuel that particularly horrific brand of nationalism. That is not to suggest that the same thing will happen in Britain, but just to point out that there are dangers. Even images of the goddess could be used in this way if she is not seen as the all-embracing force of nature but as an image who 'belongs' only to one group of people, whether they be 'Celts' or 'women', and not to others. She may, however, take particular forms that speak more to some than others. For example, the Greek goddesses may have no appeal to a black person, who could easily associate them with the cultural domination of the white West. Yet racial roots are clearly not the only factors in our choice of personally meaningful images. Many white British people relate better to Indian goddesses and gods or to native American traditions than they do to the Celtic ones. It needs to be a personal and local choice, while always holding in mind the universality of the wider reality of the goddess as life force and nature.

My own search for personally meaningful images has led me from the mysteries of Africa, where I grew up, through Egypt and ancient Greece back to the place where I have actually lived for the past 20 years, London. Always I was seeking images and sacred sites in distant places. It was a long time before I came back to where I had made my home. It was a surprising discovery. I had never felt that London was a place where the goddess lives on.

Rediscovering Avebury and Silbury Hill and other British sites was an important first step. They definitely spoke to me of ancient times, before even the Celts arrived on these isles, when the female and male principles were equally revered. Although our ideas about them must be largely speculation, they provide a powerful source of spiritual strength for women in particular and Pagans in general. I also rediscovered some very old sacred sites in the Isle of Man, where my mother lives. I connected especially strongly with some great stone monuments set on a hillside above the sea. This was while going through various painful feelings about my mother. The stones helped me to sense that I had a 'mother' who was so old and strong that she can literally go on and on and on.

Helen of London

But in the end I had to come back to London. It was while I was teaching a class on the goddess that someone told me about a community play put on locally called *Flo of the Fleet*

Figure 10.   Belonging, 1985

about the 'goddess' of the River Fleet, which is now flowing in sewers underground in London. This fascinated me, and I began to research and find out everything I could about the goddess and London.

I found a book called *The Lost Language of London* by Harold Bayley, in which he suggests that the main goddess of London before the Romans came was Ellen, or in some versions Elaine, who was pictured as a Lily maid in ancient Britain, with lilies and a basket of fruits, perhaps to represent fertility and sexuality. The similarity of her name connects her to Helen, who was both the mother of Emperor Constantine, who lived in Britain and made Christianity the official religion of the Roman world, and also the famous Helen of Troy.

With Helen of Troy we are back to yet another connection with Aphrodite, whose activities in relation to Helen started the Trojan wars. Aphrodite was the goddess chosen in a contest between her, Hera and Athena to see who was the most beautiful. Paris, a human man, was asked to make the choice and give the golden apple to the winner. So she promised him the most beautiful woman in the world, who was of course Helen. It turned out that she was already married, but, as Aphrodite planned, she fell in love with Paris. They ran off together to Troy and the Greeks sided with her wronged husband who then fought against the Trojans. The goddess Aphrodite was naturally on the side of the lovers and of Troy, which was probably still far more matricentric and goddess worshipping than most of the Greek city states that fought on the other side. They had the patriarchal goddess Athena on their side. These wars could therefore be seen as a battle between the forces of love, beauty and nature, and those of hierarchy and glorification of war.

Maybe once, long ago, London too was on the side of love, beauty and nature, rather than a centre from which men have gone out to conquer the world. Indeed, there are some interesting connections between London and Troy. Pre-Roman myth tells of London being founded by Brutus, who was supposed to have come from Troy after the famous wars.

In fact it was called Troy Novant, or the New Troy, when the Romans first arrived.

Helen is also mentioned in the *Mabinogion*, a medieval history of Britain: it is said that when the Romans came to Britain and wanted roads built across the country, the local men would only build them for Helen, so she must have been an important deity for them. In Wales some of these roads are actually still called Sarn Helen. There are even stories suggesting that the Roman leaders in Britain could rule only if they were seen by the 'natives' as being married to Helen or Ellen, or perhaps, as in the case of Constantine, were her 'son'.

In another story St Helen is the daughter of King Cole, famous in the nursery rhyme. Alfred Watkins, who 'discovered' ley lines (which are 'lines' of energy running through the landscape, often connecting ancient sacred sites), points out that the name 'Cole' apparently meant light or splendour in ancient Britain. This gave King Cole (and Helen) a connection with the lines themselves and with the sites that they linked. She was perhaps representative of the *principle of interconnectedness* of nature in general and of centres of sacred energy and learning in particular. Even Helen's name has a link with the Semitic word *El*, which means light or luminous one, and was an early name in the Near East for God.

In their pamphlet *Elen Goddess of Nature*, Caroline Munro and Chesca Potter argue that she represented a kind of primeval force of nature, much as Aphrodite must once have done. They say that 'stories of Elen seem to encode mysteries of female sexual energy'. They even suggest that the Templars, who were a medieval religious order that traditional Christians feared greatly, used to 'work this force'.

In Sparta, a classical-Greek city state, there used to be a festival called the Helenophoria, which had strong sexual connotations. Phallic and other sexual symbols would be carried in baskets, which probably represented the womb and vagina. The special basket was even called a 'helene'. She was apparently seen there as an orgiastic deity, which fits in with the theory that she represented that very powerful and primordial force that is the deep nature of female sexuality. It is, of course, also Eros and indeed the kind of love that makes the whole universe go round. This same energy can also be found within the Earth, concentrated at particular points or along particular lines similar to ley lines. Perhaps it could be described as a kind of electrical energy or as the serpents within the Earth.

In Rhodes, Helen was a fertility goddess, and was worshipped in the form of dolls hanging from a tree. Her association with trees continued in the myth that St Helen went to the Holy Land and discovered the true cross on which Jesus was hung. Trees are very powerful images of the round of nature, as well as having strong energies, perhaps of the same kind as ley lines and female sexuality. In Rhodes she was worshipped in the form of little dolls hanging from trees, as were Ariadne and Inanna. There is here a life-and-death motif, perhaps connected to the actual hanging of criminals or sacrificial victims on trees, or the gentler idea of leaves on trees growing and dying while the trunk and branches continue slowly to grow. But there may be something else. The act of swinging can itself be very sexual and can even lead into quite a powerful trance state. Traditionally little girls have used swings more than boys. It could be that they were used in rituals to enhance this same electrical, sexual, spiritual energy that we have been describing earlier. And Helen/Ellen was the personification of that energy.

Helen is also associated with a number of holy wells, rivers and streams, both in Britain and elsewhere. As the principle of flow that permeates the whole universe, water itself represents a sacred force. As our bodies are largely made up of water we can often feel special and strong inner connections with water, especially in its natural state. But where water wells up from beneath the surface of the earth there is a particularly beautiful image of the waters of the mother's body coming out through her vagina. These could be the sexual waters of her arousal as well as the waters breaking before she gives birth. But there is also, as I have experienced myself, a very electrically charged energy around many of those ancient wells. This could be the result of thousands of years of people worshipping at such places, which were and sometimes still are seen as sacred.

I like to think that the spirit of Helen lives on under the city streets of London. Although nearly all the wells are now blocked up and the rivers turned into sewers, the energy that she represented is still there.

The River Fleet was once called the River of Wells. Many of these were blocked up only in the last 100 or so years. They have wonderful names like 'Black Mary's Hole', which clearly conjures up female sexual symbolism. Helen can also be associated with the serpent power that is described as kundalini in India and actually exists in our bodies as primal sexual energy. The River Thames looks very serpent-like in its form, and one of the London tributaries now forms the Serpentine Lake. The rest of that river is now underground. The Thames itself is still called the Isis in Oxford, which suggests clear goddess associations. In some ways Isis, the Egyptian goddess, represents similar primeval energies to Helen. And there was apparently a temple to Isis in London during the Roman occupation.

After all this research I wanted to experience for myself the sense of Helen's energies in the hidden waters beneath the city. One of the most famous sacred wells in London, now blocked up, was next to St Bride's Church near the bend in the old River Fleet, where it flows under Fleet Street and turns down towards the Thames at Blackfriars. The site is almost certainly a pre-Roman one and down in the crypt of the church one can feel the kind of sacred, sexual, electrical energies that Helen represents. St Bride was, after all, a Christianized version of the old goddess Brigantia who, like Helen, was associated with light. She was also a goddess of healing, fire and wisdom. Both goddesses seem to have this connection with spiritual light, the pure energy of which we are all a part. Both are also associated with water and the flow of life, wells, springs and

Figure 11.   Waters of the Gap, Sulis, 1987

places that link two worlds, perhaps the underworld and the overworld, and the sacred passages between life and death.

The first time I ever visited St Bride's church was with a small group of women from the class I teach on the goddess. We all felt the energy down in the crypt, but were sad not to be able to see the old well itself. However, when we left and walked down Fleet Street, suddenly in front of us all this water began to bubble out from under the pavement. It was like magic. Helen was telling us all that she was indeed still here. Of course, on one level it was simply a burst water-pipe, but why did it start pouring out just at the very moment we arrived? We were all amazed. Some of us jumped into the water and splashed it around ourselves, our faith in the goddess renewed once more.

Names and Identities

In the same way that connections with and love of place can be used to create or preserve hierarchies, so can our personal identities and names. It is important to explore ways of linking with our ancestors *without* becoming racist or divided from our fellow human beings who have different ones. Many people on their journeys of self-discovery have had to break away from families, communities and from their whole backgrounds. These are often completely rejected at first, even despised. But returning to our roots, rediscovering their positive aspects and relating to our parents again are all important parts of the process for many of us.

One way of doing this in the context of the ancient goddesses and gods is through our names. Exploring the names that we were given at birth may be a vital first step before, or even instead of, changing them, as some people do today. In the Christian tradition, for example, many people are given the names of saints, such as Mary or Anne. Often these saints' names have originally come from pagan roots, which tend to have far more powerful and wider meanings.

I personally found that, as I worked with thoughts and feelings around the goddesses of London, one name kept cropping up in my mind. The name was El-anna, just a slightly different version of Ellen or Elaine. It somehow felt more ancient and universal, perhaps less English! I had always felt myself to be an international and even classless person, and coming back to rediscover England, my parents and my background was not easy. Then I remembered that my middle name is Anne. So I began to explore the ancient roots of that name. The root Ana comes up in the names of many ancient Middle Eastern goddesses such as Anath, Anat, Di-Ana and Anatha (mentioned in the Bible generally as evil), and in the Celtic tradition too as Danu, Anu or Nanna. It almost seems to be a universal name for the oldest mother of all, the one who might be represented by grandmothers as an archetypal group. Anne was, of course, the grandmother of Jesus in the Bible. This is likely to be a story that goes back many thousands of years, in which Ana is always the oldest female ancestor behind the scenes. It is also probably one of the earliest sounds that a baby makes, and it has a very primeval feel to it.

The Romans called her Anna Perenna, 'Eternal Anna', the one who stands at the gates or doors when one year or time phase moves into the next. She is both looking forwards and looking backwards. She is both the beginning and the end. She was also Jana or Juno, the mother of the January New Year. Interestingly for me, my birthday is on New Year's Day and I often have a sense of living on the borders between things, acutely aware of the opposites and paradoxes of life. So for me, the goddess of London and of the place where I am in the here and now is El-anna.

In classes and workshops where I have worked with people on reconnections with place and names, everyone has found similar kinds of links. Sometimes we have also looked at street names and found connections with ancient goddesses or gods. Harold Bayley's *The Lost Language of London* is a useful, albeit imaginative, source for exploring the street and area names of

Figure 12. El-Anna, 1989

London. I live next to a road called Ellingham Road, and like to think of ancient connections with Ellen of London. There was, until 100 years ago, a stream running beside the road, and long ago all streams were seen as sacred and as 'residences' of the goddess. She was often known as the spirit of the place and may have had different names at specific places, as well as more general titles. Even though there may be little direct archaeological evidence it can be fun to speculate and imagine one's back garden as an old sacred space, for example. Many people are sensitive to underground water, which is often present beneath the homes in which we live our daily lives. And all water can be seen as sacred, as an expression of the goddess.

All these are ways of experiencing the local, the particular and the personal as linked to the universal, to the whole of nature, to mother earth. This kind of linking does not require that we go through any specific family or group or religion. We can let go of belonging to or being possessed by one particular group, just because we were born into it.

Earth/Body Connections

As a psychotherapist I work a lot with people's relations to their mothers. And this personal work is vitally important. But we need to take the individual experience and connect it to the universal fact that all of us came from a woman's womb, usually through the vagina. The vagina is a universal sacred image, of which personal examples are representatives. The womb is a sacred place. And for all women, whether we give birth to children or not, that place in our bodies has a special relationship to the goddess, to the earth. It is a place of source from which all things must come. And we are privileged to carry these sacred sites around with us wherever we go. We could even think of our vaginas and wombs as shrines or temples, hidden and protected from the outside world — places we can go to in meditation when we need to reconnect with the divine.

Focusing attention on the womb area of our bodies, even for men, is a way of bringing energy down from the head, in which most of us are engrossed. It can be very calming. Placing a hand over it can help to remind us. Breathing right down into it can be like taking in the love energy of the goddess, bringing her home to the place where she belongs. The out-breath can be like letting go of the fear that may be creating a barrier to the 'temple' in the solar plexus or heart areas.

To reinforce the image of womb as sacred site, the whole menstrual cycle can be seen as a spiritual ritual. The time of bleeding is a time of sacrifice, letting go of the egg that could have become a baby, letting go of tensions and fears that may have built up. The pouring out of blood can be experienced as a time of great power and sexual energy, our red time. People may be especially attracted to us at this time. It is a holy time. We may often feel like going into ourselves, thinking, staying in bed, having others look after us. Then comes the energy increase at ovulation in the middle of the cycle, when many women feel highly sexual and want to go out into the world and express themselves. Dancing, love-making and creative work are ways of using this energy that could, biologically, go into conception. Instead, other ideas, projects, friendships may be conceived at this time.

Of course, women vary a lot in how their cycles work and may be affected by the moon as well. Full moon would be the 'appropriate' time for ovulation and the dark of the moon for bleeding. Menstruation and responses to the moon are yet other ways in which the individual is linked to the universal. Many women living closely together will actually bleed together. 'Chemistry' links us in subtle ways.

So for me celebrating the 'rites of El-anna' does not require going to any temple or church, but simply being fully alive in my own body. This is not at all easy for a person like me who has always lived so much in the head. There are a number of ways that I have found and am exploring, along with many other women and some men, to really put into practice what we mean when we say the body is sacred.

Because I see El-anna as related to Helen, Aphrodite and Ishtar, she especially represents love and/or sexual energy. We can feel this energy within us without the presence of a lover in various ways. These are some of the ways that I have found to be effective:

1. Putting all our attention into parts of the body, one at a time, perhaps starting with the feet, until we can feel it tingling. Eventually our whole bodies will feel full of streaming energy, golden light, love.
2. Sending compassionate love from the heart into ourselves, imagining 'pouring' it onto our bodies. We may want to hug and/or caress ourselves. We may choose to imagine ourselves as a child being loved by ourselves as adults.
3. Focusing on our genitals and letting ourselves feel aroused, excited, then 'pouring' that energy through ourselves, feeling it as the goddess rising from our womb and vaginal areas to infuse our whole bodies. We can take it down our legs and feel it in our feet, or take it up our spines and over our heads. When we do this, anywhere — on the street, at home, on the bus — we can experience it as being with the goddess or having her within us. There is no need to *do* anything about it: we don't have to rush off and find a lover, just stay with it and enjoy the feeling. We may want to express it further by loosening the pelvic area and swinging our hips as we walk, for example. Or we may want to dance, alone or with others. But it can be enjoyed in stillness too.

We can take this 'goddess' anywhere that we go. But some people also like to have special places where this feeling can be especially strong. These may be sacred sites or favourite outdoor spots like parks, or they may be indoors, a bedroom or a shrine in a corner of the living-room for example.

4. Making shrines has become more and more common, although many people would not use the word. Often on a mantelpiece one sees a few stones, plants or crystals. These are examples of specific local objects representing the mother nature as a whole. Others set up more sophisticated shrines, perhaps with candles and pictures or statues of favourite goddesses or gods. Some people carry out rituals at these shrines, but there need be nothing more than a respect for the objects, perhaps sometimes lighting a candle, maybe meditating on it or on the objects simply by focusing attention on them. Prayers may be made to the goddess or god and thanks given for life gifts from them. Talking to them as a friend about life's ups and downs may be enough. A mirror might also be useful to look at oneself and the divine within, to learn to love oneself and to see through into the soul behind the face.

5. As well as simple focusing meditations at the shrine it is also a good place to send out compassionate love towards those whom we love, and sometimes it's good 'training' to send it to people we are neutral about or even hate. Practising the sending of compassionate love is probably one of the most important aspects of living with the goddesses of love. Notice that I don't use the word 'worship', for that implies looking up to something outside, while she lives in our hearts and wombs and, in fact, all over our bodies.

How do we use these ideas in everyday life and relationships? Some examples from people's experience can point the way.

Margaret had been looking after her elderly mother for many years. Her mother had become increasingly difficult and demanding and Margaret felt increasingly resentful. When her mother criticized, which she frequently did, Margaret felt like a child again inside and experienced her mother as all powerful. In therapy she learnt to think differently about her mother, seeing her now as frail and dependent, afraid and powerless. She needed to go to the opposite extreme of how she had seen her mother before, in order to achieve more balance. When her mother was thought of in such different terms it was easier for Margaret to take back all her projections onto the old woman, which actually came from many years before, when she was a child.

But the most important, the most difficult part of her therapy was learning to feel compassionate love towards her mother. She had to practise every day, several times a day, just imaging her mother in her mind, small and frail, and then beaming love from the heart towards that image. At first she couldn't do it all. There was too much anger in the way. To get that out of the way, Margaret was encouraged to write down all her resentments and her appreciations of her mother. By keeping on one side all the good things she felt, she was able to really let rip with all the resentments. Then she was more able to get in touch with the compassionate love. Before this work in therapy, Margaret had been going to church and trying to say prayers for her mother, feeling terribly guilty about her anger but unable to access genuine love, only a kind of 'duty love'. In therapy she was allowed to have the anger which made the love more available. Instead of praying to an external god, she now practised sending this genuine, compassionate love as her main spiritual activity. It came more and more from her body, not just from her head.

Fiona had been going out with Kevin for about a year. At first it had been very passionate and loving. They fell in love while on holiday in Italy and were practically inseparable when they returned to London. But this stage lasted only a couple of months and then Kevin began to be increasingly busy at work, and started to put her down and make her jealous by flirting at parties. He claimed he was still in love with her and certainly did not want to let her go. The relationship began to make Fiona unhappy, but she did not leave because the bond they had created in those first two months was so strong that it seemed to her that they were made for each other.

She clung on to this romantic belief for a long time. As she got to know Kevin better she discovered that he had had a very smothering mother who had poured all her sexual energy onto him as the only son. While a part of him was always looking to replace his mother and merge with some new woman, he also had a terror of being dominated, so had to withdraw and be separate after a while. Therapy helped them both to understand this pattern.

But while Fiona pretended to herself that she now understood and accepted him, underneath she was furious. She tried to love him unconditionally and be like the new-age books she was reading told her she should be. But this was a love from the head, not from the body. The body was angry. Eventually in her own therapy she contacted that anger, and raged at him, physically hitting cushions and writing letters that she didn't send. After this she was better able to see the situation clearly in terms of her own needs and decided to end it. But she also practised visualizing him and sending compassionate love from the heart. This only worked after the anger was expressed, and it needed a lot of concentration. She found it helpful to practise at the same time sending compassionate love to other people in her life. Eventually this became her main meditation practice and she began to be able to beam compassionate love out towards strangers in the city at will.

Simon was very involved with healing and meditation. His work was acupuncture and yoga teaching. He thought that he was very much a 'new man', and in touch with his body. And yet he found himself frequently obsessed with sexual fantasies and desires for women he saw in the street. These bothered him so much that he began to wonder whether he really did love the girlfriend he had been with for three years. The feelings seemed to be completely out of his control.

And that issue of control turned out to be the problem. All his 'spiritual' work had actually been geared towards *controlling* the body and especially its 'baser' instincts. Even the Eastern philosophies that he followed supported this approach to the body. In therapy Simon learnt to accept and celebrate his own sexuality. He began slowly to enjoy the sexual feelings he had around women in the street, knowing he did not have to do anything about them. He could control his actions, but he did not need to control the sensations totally.

It also came out that he was very controlling in bed with his girlfriend, thinking that this was the way he was supposed to be. Gradually he began simply to watch his own body and its reactions without having to control them. He noticed all the different sensations he experienced at different points in love-making and became less goal orientated. But he also learnt to think differently about sex and bodies in general. As he accepted his own sexuality more he became less threatened by his girlfriend and sometimes let her take the lead. He started a practice of looking in a full-length mirror everyday and telling each part of his body how much he loves it. This proves to be a good balance for him in contrast to the rest of his meditation, which was in the head. He also began to let go in other areas too, for example taking more holidays and being less of a workaholic.

Jill came into therapy because she was doing a course on counselling. She didn't really think that she needed it. She had been married for ten years, divorced for four. She had not had a relationship since leaving her husband. At first Jill insisted that she was quite happy with the situation, as she had a very high-powered job in the City and really didn't have time for a man. Gradually, however, it turned out that she had never really been in touch with her own sexuality, coming from a repressed upper-class background and believing that it was all about pleasing the man. Her husband had basically abused her, emotionally and sexually, and she was really scared of her own sexuality. In therapy Jill talked about how powerful her early sexual feelings had been in her teens. But then her first experience in the back of a car had been so awful that she began to shut them off. After that she always did just what the man wanted.

It took a long time for Jill to believe deeply that her sexual feelings were good and her own. Reading books on the goddess and feminism helped her in this change of belief. She also worked on loving her body and allowing herself sexual fantasies. By concentrating on her own sexuality, while she was not even in a sexual relationship with a man, she was able to see it as her own, not only something that arises in response to someone else. She began to watch through the month at what times she felt especially sexual. This energy became seen as a gift from the goddess to be enjoyed and celebrated. Eventually she joined a group of women who celebrate the full moons and the eight major pagan festivals with ritual and celebration, including naked dancing.

Pauline had been sexually abused as a child by her father. She always felt that sex and her body were something dirty and that she was bad. She had had many sexual relationships but always secretly despised herself and the men. Basically she hated her own body. In therapy a lot of work was done with the rage against her father, but a point then came when she wanted to move on. First she had to somehow purify or even consecrate her own body, make it sacred once again. With her friends she devised her own ritual, using incense and salt water to purify and banish the negative energy. She then visualized her body as a temple and the goddess as pure loving light entering it and filling her from within. She was held and loved by friends to show that not all humans are brutal and invasive. In the end she was able to form a more satisfying relationship with a man, but only after she got him also to make his body a temple like hers and to dedicate himself to the goddess, only entering when it felt absolutely right. In fact they did not have intercourse for the first few months of their relationship. Pauline now had a deep respect for her body and a sense of timing and 'rightness' about sexual relationships.

While many people have found that a focus on their own bodies can help not only in solving emotional, psychological problems, but also in contacting a deeper kind of spirituality, others find their healing outside in nature first. Joan, who had grown up in the country, was very lonely in the city and found little solace in her local church. So she would go and sit by a particular tree every day. The tree became like her mother and after a while she began to talk (under her breath) to the tree. At first she thought that she was going mad. But then in a group of women exploring goddess spirituality she discovered that she was not mad at all. She stopped going to church altogether and went instead for walks in the woods, and learnt about goddesses like Artemis, who represent the 'wilder' side of women. Although she did not have any sexual relationship she began to think of trees as her lovers. She could eventually actually feel their energy in her body whenever she needed to, branches and limbs entwining her, entering her, being her.

Carlos had come to London from Brazil and could find nothing of his own religion, African based, in this city. Then he began to search for that same energy in the clubs and meeting places of the city, creating his own personal religion of dance and trance. He happened to go to a class on mythology and discovered the links between his own beloved Imanja, the African goddess of the sea, and Aphrodite and Helen. Places where there was water in the city soon became places to commune with Imanja. He found the river an especially comforting place after this discovery, and would often go and sit by the river quietly praying to his goddess from home, whom he realized was of course here too, just going by a different name.

5

Oshun and Yemaya of Africa

RECONNECTING WITH THE BLACK GODDESS

All too often love, in whatever form, is reserved for people who are of a similar social and/or ethnic group. Interracial marriages, for example, are still rare and frowned on throughout the world. Yet if we are going to have a truly international world there needs to be a far deeper and genuine ability to love people of other races and backgrounds. It is not enough simply to be tolerant or concerned. These feelings smack of a patronizing and superior attitude. And once again our internalized mythology and imagery around race play a major role in preserving the stereotypes and racist beliefs from which such surface attitudes come. Struggles to change these images have been going on for decades. But some of the most powerful, influential and difficult to change are the religious images. Jesus is still generally portrayed as white, for example, and when portrayed as black it is often in the context of black or mixed congregations. What about an all-white church 'worshipping' a black Jesus? Only when changes in imagery are widespread enough to be part of mainstream culture will society really begin to change. But perhaps by then the whole idea of 'worship' and 'church' will be transformed.

The goddess as a generalized image is still generally portrayed as white, although there are many exceptions. And the world of goddess spirituality, especially in the United States, is far more conscious of racism than the world of conventional Christianity. Many white women, as well as black, are visioning black goddesses, but even here there are dangers of stereotyping. Black goddesses who are seen as 'closer to raw nature' or more sexual or even more motherly fit in all too easily with white stereotypes of the 'black mama' or 'black seductress'. So we need constantly to question our own unconscious programming.

The black goddess is, however, a rising image in the modern unconscious. She can have many meanings and take many forms. She visits us in our dreams and in our waking hours as dark, devouring Kali of India, as the black madonna of countless European churches, and as Imanja, swirling in the back streets of Brazilian cities. For many she has no particular form and may be a slim, dancing figure or a large and stately lady, a child or a crone.

But what is especially interesting about the black goddess is that she has never really disappeared, as most of the others have. She has been kept alive throughout the era of Christianity and the patriarchal abhorrence of the female. She has continued quietly working in the background, changing shape and form to fit in with the needs of the time. She has always been alive in Africa, despite the same changes towards patriarchal religion that have taken place elsewhere. Generally she started as the source of everything, then a consort or son would appear who would eventually take over as supreme. As with the Greeks, cultures such as the Yoruba and the Ashanti of Nigeria and Ghana respectively seem to have evolved in this way towards patriarchy, even before the Islamic and Christian influences speeded up the process.

So even in Africa we are not dealing with a 'pure' goddess tradition. To find this we would have to go back to pre-dynastic Egypt, Libya and the long-lost cultures of the once-fertile Sahara. Here we would be talking about a time of around 5000 BC. It is likely that African peoples from these early goddess cultures moved into the Nile valley when their lands dried up and influenced the beginnings of what we call civilizations such as the Egyptian and Greek ones.

There is archeological evidence that in Catal Huyuk, a goddess-centred city in Anatolia *circa* 6000 BC, there was a very racially mixed population with a majority described as Afro-Europeans. No doubt the world in those days had very different racial mixes and probably very different ideas and images around race. It is likely that concepts of racial inferiority are a product of the more general hierarchical thinking that goes hand in hand with patriarchy and the domination of nature. It may not have become so deeply entrenched as it is today until the times of capitalist expansion from the seventeenth century onwards. Humans may always have been afraid of or curious about people different from themselves, but even today children do not automatically fear or put down someone of a different colour. Rigid colour hierarchies are socially constructed and not biologically given.

The colour black may have been a particularly sacred colour. Some of the earliest representations of the goddess were black stones, possibly meteorites like the stone at Mecca hidden in the holiest shrine there. And in Europe the black madonnas seem to have a more powerful feeling to them than the more common white ones. They are almost always given extra reverence. Whether this is due to a deep folk memory of some long-forgotten original black goddess or to ideas such as the sacredness of fire and the black colour that everything turns when burnt, we can only guess.

Whatever ancient black goddesses were once revered in Africa thousands of years ago, we do know that in her more recent form she was brought, along with the slaves, to the New World over the last few hundred years. The forms that she had in places like Nigeria as Oshun and Yemaya were used directly by the slaves in their new 'homes'. Even her names were often kept. It is remarkable, given the efforts that the slave owners made to squash any remains of African culture or identity, that she has been kept so very vibrantly alive to this day. In many places, such as Brazil and the Caribbean islands, she was cleverly merged with the Virgin Mary. Yet unlike in Christianity, her rituals were mainly carried out by women.

Today in the religions of Macumba (Brazil) and Santeria (Puerto Rico, Cuba, USA) and the many other African-derived traditions it is mainly female priestesses who dress up in the flowing white and blue of Imanja (another name for Yemaya) and perform her rituals on the sea shore or in tiny city apartments crowded with her images, candles and cowrie shells. There are, of course, the African male gods too, such as Shango, and men are rarely excluded, but the overwhelming impression is one of enormous female power of a kind rarely experienced in the Christian or Islamic traditions.

While thousands of women and men are looking to the past to find the goddess, amongst the ruins of Greece or in the silent stones of Malta, she is still alive in the Black Diaspora just round the corner, in New York, in Rio, in Mexico City and even in London. But this religion is still seen as not quite respectable, still the religion of slaves, still a guilty secret, still a religion of the poor, a superstitious cult. Yet it may be that there is more potential here for a healing of the racial and other splits in our world than in all the do-gooding of the Christian church. For here is a genuinely female energy being revered. And while the love of Christianity is an intellectual sort of love about care and concern for the downtrodden, the love of Oshun and Yemaya is a deeply physical love from the body, from the roots of one's being. It is the love of a mother for the child that grew in her body, the ecstasy of sexual love, the direct use of love energy in healing; it is a love that shakes the whole body to its core.

The African Love Goddesses

Oshun and Yemaya are of particular importance to this book as they are goddesses of love. They are also two of the most powerful and familiar goddesses of the New World African religion. Both come from the Yoruba tradition in Nigeria and they are usually seen as two separate goddesses: Yemaya is associated with the sea and Oshun with rivers. They are both

Figure 13. Yemaya, 1989

personifications of water, of strong feelings, of sexuality, of love. This association with water and love connects them to Aphrodite, Elen, Venus and countless others. They have a very direct association with nature and with ourselves, too, if we remember that we are also largely made up of water.

Yemaya is sometimes depicted as a mermaid, a powerful image in so many traditions. The fish's tail may help to remind us that a part of us is still immersed in our ancient, fish-like selves, responding to the call of the oceans in an instinctual, spontaneous way, despite our developed brains. A part of us is still swimming in the unconscious. The mermaid can also remind us of where we came from, as individuals out of the waters of our mothers' wombs, and as a species out of the sea where life first formed. The mermaid is also sometimes seen, especially in patriarchy, as a seductress. She may lead men into depths that are too frightening to handle, too demanding, too changeable.

Yemaya is the sea, the source, the great mother from whom all else in creation came. In one Yoruba story she has already been demoted from her original role by being the daughter of Obatala, a kind of African Zeus, a father figure. She had a son called Orungun who became more and more macho and aggressive as he grew older, until eventually he raped his own mother. This could be symbolic of the male takeover in Yoruba society. She cursed her son or, in another version, lured him into the sea to drown. But when she had done this vengeance, she was filled with remorse and began to weep for the son she had lost. This is reminiscent of Inanna's mourning for Dumuzi. She went up to the top of the highest mountain in the land and there she died while giving birth to the fourteen Yoruba goddesses and gods. The waters from her womb caused a great flood all over the world, and she also gave birth to the first human beings, so the sense of her as ultimate source has remained in these stories. The place where she died is called Ile Ife and is a sacred city to this very day. Perhaps her death also symbolized the death of the goddess as the all-powerful main deity.

Yemaya is still 'worshipped' in the Santeria religion as very much alive, present and powerful. Sometimes she is merged with the Virgin Mary as Our Lady of Regla or Star of the Sea. She is associated with childbirth and women pray to her to have children. In Santeria she is usually portrayed wearing white with blue beads. She is large, beautiful and stately. She takes care of the home, the womb and children. Yet she is not just a mother goddess. She is also associated with the moon. She is mysterious and profound. Above all, she is compassionate. She is the one who will go on caring when life is difficult, when dangerous tasks are to be performed. She watches over people. She is like the Virgin Mary, but somehow more powerful, more fertile, more sexual. Her symbols are boats, flowers, sea shells and fans. On 1 February, in Bahia, Brazil, her priestesses go down to the sea and send out little boats filled with white roses to float off as offerings to her and to bring them good fortune for the coming year. If they return to the beach this is seen as a bad sign. It is interesting to note the date, which is the same as Imbolc in the Celtic calendar, the day of Bride (or Bridgit), another goddess of light, love and healing.

Oshun, like Ishtar and Aphrodite, is the sacred harlot. She is called Mistress Erzulie in Haiti, where she was called upon by the slave revolt led by Tousant l'Ouvuture in the nineteenth century. She gave them the strength and courage to fight. She is a very powerful goddess. She is love in its most sensual, sexual form. She is desire itself. She is the urge to merge. She is the African Eros. She is sometimes described as Yemaya's daughter, but usually the two goddesses are more like sisters. She is represented as a beautiful dancer, with lots of jewellery, especially bracelets that jingle as she moves. She is a kind of enchantress, seducing everyone into the pleasures of love.

In the Yoruba stories she has a reputation, like Aphrodite, for having lots of affairs. She is married to Orunmula, who is a wise old man, but she gets bored and becomes interested in Ogun, whom she seduces. She is found out and exposed, but somehow forgiven. Her sexuality is under no man's

control. And she hates to be bored. Another of her lovers is
Shango. Ogun and Shango are the gods of war and thunder.
Their liaisons with Oshun remind one, like Aphrodite's affair
with Ares, of the connection between love and war. 'All is fair
in love and war.'

Another story about Oshun tells how she learnt divining,
which is seeing into the future by throwing cowrie shells and
reading the patterns. In patriarchal Yoruba tradition only
Obatala, the father god, knew the art of divining. Oshun kept
pleading with him to teach her, but he always refused. One
day he went to the river to bathe. He took off his clothes and
left them on the bank. Then along came Elegba, who is a kind
of trickster god, who stole the clothes and ran off home.
Oshun was walking along by the river picking flowers when
she saw Obatala swimming naked. On seeing her he felt
embarrassed and rushed to get his clothes. But, of course, they
were gone. So Oshun made him an offer. She told him that
if he taught her the art of divining she would find his clothes
for him. Oshun had seen Elegba carry them off, so she walked
fast to his house, just pausing to make herself as beautiful as
possible. Like Aphrodite she could be quite irresistible. Indeed,
when Elegba saw her, he desired her desperately. She
demanded the clothes he had stolen. Perhaps promising to
sleep with him some other time, she eventually persuaded him
to part with the clothes. Overjoyed, Oshun rushed back to the
river, and there and then Obatala taught her all the secrets of
shell divining.

Oshun might seem at first to represent exactly the kind of
woman feminists despise, someone who uses her sexual power
to get things out of the patriarchy without trying to change
it. She appears to be manipulative rather than directly
assertive. And yet this is so often the only way that women
have been able to get what they want or even get what it is
their right to have. It is likely that in earlier Yoruba culture,
as in most others, the art of divination was originally a female
preserve. So Oshun is merely taking back what is rightfully
hers. And besides, the art of trickery has always been a vital

tool for the oppressed, not to be despised, but rather admired for the ingenuity so often required. The Ananse stories originating from Ghana went with the slaves to the New World and are all about a spiderman who, though smaller and weaker than other animals, was always able to outwit the others. Indeed, the archetype of the trickster appears in most cultures, as Hermes or Mercury, for example, in the West. In the Yoruba tradition he is Elegba.

Oshun does not only use trickery, but also her very considerable sexual power. This may also seem to be unfair to other women who are not so beautiful. But if we see her in a most abstract way she is actually an embodiment, albeit a stereotyped one, of the energy that is available to anyone. She is a force of nature, she is pure sexuality, she is the power of love, love for others and for oneself. This energy is not the prerogative of beautiful women. Many small girls and boys enjoy displaying their own bodies with no shame or ideas about beauty and ugliness, which are largely socially constructed mental concepts anyway. It is this joy in one's own body, in one's own sexual energy, in one's own natural powerfulness that Oshun represents. We need to look beyond the image created by patriarchy to the energy behind her.

Modern women, both black and white, are especially linked by the media ideals of beauty. We often fail to really love ourselves if we don't 'match up'. And as very few of us do fit, there are millions of women desperately trying to look totally different, even going to such extremes as plastic surgery in order to change. There is almost an epidemic of diet-related illnesses, such as anorexia. As Naomi Wolf pointed out in her book *The Beauty Myth*, this obsession with looks, which the patriarchy has encouraged ever since the 1960s when women began to have more power, is now keeping us back. Always we are trying to fit in with an external image. Always we are thinking in terms of how others see us. And many even believe deep down that they will only be loved if they look a certain way, for ever searching for an external source of what is within.

Today we need the real Oshun more than ever. To bring her back into our lives is to revive the lost girl (or boy) in all of us, the girl who loves being in her body, who loves her own sexual sensations and who delights in exhibitionism. To return to Oshun is to give ourselves permission to show off, to honour that hidden side of most, if not all women, the side that secretly longs to display itself, to be a show off, even to be outrageous. In places like Britain, especially, showing off is about the worst thing that anyone can do. Our achievements, looks, ability are supposed to be played down. Even boys and men suffer from this. But for girls it is seen as particularly dangerous, because exhibitionism of the body might attract men who would then not be able to control themselves and the woman would deserve to be raped or worse. The myth is kept alive by social attitudes about men being uncontrollable beasts and women 'asking for it' if they dress a certain way.

And in other areas of life women are taught not to show off, or even excel, because then they would not be able to find and keep a man, which is of course seen as the most important thing in life! Women are not supposed to be selfish but always to put others first. Oshun tells us otherwise. She encourages us to love ourselves passionately, to take care of ourselves, to give ourselves treats and sometimes even to put ourselves first, before others. It isn't a crime.

Indeed, loving ourselves helps us to love others more. It's when we don't love ourselves enough that we grudge giving love or even admiration to others. We are more likely to resent or envy other people. Deep self-love is very different from arrogance or egotism, narcissism or self-obsession, all of which could be described as neurotic patterns, often arising as compensation for insecurity or shame. Deep self-love can be shared with others, while egotism is focused entirely on the self and involves a blindness and lack of interest in the other person.

Yet if there has been too much emphasis on other people, a person may need to go through a stage when they do seem to be egotistic. For women especially this may be a vital part of their personal journey. After attending assertion-training classes many women go back to families who complain bitterly that mum has now become selfish. She is no longer behaving like the family servant. And some people do overdo it, as a reaction to the way they were before.

For many women and some men their spiritual journey needs to include not only losing the ego, but also developing one in the first place. When I was in my twenties I floated around with very little ego, being 'spiritual' but letting people put me down and use me, all over the place. After that I had to develop a stronger ego, a sense of self, to create 'myself' in a way. I had to learn to value my achievements more and boast, even. Then came the harder but deeper task of true self-loving, which I am still working with.

Below I include some ways that I and others have found useful in the process of learning to love ourselves. And throughout this process, Oshun has been quietly working away in the background. She is especially appropriate for me, as my first models for self-loving people were in Africa where I grew up as a child. But she is a useful and powerful image for anyone, black or white.

Self-Loving

Physical Self-Loving

Prepare yourself with a long, hot bath, with oils or whatever else you like to pamper yourself with. Baths often feature in myths of the goddess as ways of renewing virginity or purifying the body. Today we need once again to understand the true meaning of virginity as being 'a woman unto herself' or 'a woman who belongs to herself not to anyone else' or 'a woman who is complete in herself'. It does not mean a woman who has never had intercourse with a man. Climbing out of the bath can be a moment savoured as a new beginning, a starting afresh.

Then find a full-length mirror, light a candle or two, and just stand in front of it admiring yourself. Any judgements about bits of your body that you don't like can be noticed but then let go of. In a dim and mysterious light such as candlelight it may be easier for some of us to believe we are beautiful. Tell yourself several times that you are beautiful. You could tell your mirror image that you love her. Then you could stroke different parts of your body, caress yourself, hug yourself, touch yourself wherever it feels good. This can be a very empowering experience, and the more often you can do it, the better you are likely to feel about yourself. It could, of course, lead into masturbation and a longer, more sexual kind of self-loving with whatever fantasies are appropriate.

Mental Self-Loving

On a large sheet of paper write down everything that you can think of that is positive about yourself. All your achievements, good qualities, abilities. It is surprising how difficult many women especially find this to do. They often leave out obvious qualities that everyone else notices.

Then think about areas in your life where you would like to feel better or more confident, and write down sentences starting with 'I am . . .' as if you already were like you want to be. These affirmations can then be repeated every day until you begin to believe them. It may seem artificial at first, but it can work. I saw a client the other day who had been using the affirmation 'I am worthy of respect', and after a couple of weeks she was actually behaving differently to people who had previously put her down, telling them what she really thought. You could also just tell yourself from time to time during the day that you love yourself, perhaps putting your name first, as in 'Anne, I love you.'

Emotional Self-Loving

The affirmations and words of love can lead on to a deeper emotional self-loving. This can include imaging oneself and sending loving energy from the heart to that image. The energy can simply be recycled back into the self while giving oneself a hug or touching one's own heart. You could also visualize yourself at different ages or use a photograph to send love to. Many of us have been hurt as small children and didn't feel loved enough just for ourselves. We could imagine putting ourselves as small children on our own adult knees and cuddling ourselves.

A rather strange idea, which I personally found useful, is to symbolically 'marry' oneself. This is different from 'marrying' one's Eros or an imagined spiritual 'other'. It involves a focus of love and commitment towards the self. It can be done alone or with others, depending on how imaginative your friends are. I did it alone in the woods one New Year's Eve. It is important to find the right place and time: a birthday is a good time, for example. You could actually get dressed up and even prepare a feast. The ritual can be whatever you decide is appropriate. You could give yourself a ring, necklace, whatever, to symbolize the event. Basically you are affirming your love for yourself, perhaps repeating it several times solemnly, and then you make promises to yourself, such as 'I promise to support and honour you for the rest of my life.' You could make up a whole list of promises to the self.

Social Self-Loving

Going out into the world loving oneself can be hardest of all if we are used to patterns of low self-esteem. It is important first to be clear about one's own needs in every situation and then to ask for them to be met, while respecting the other person's reality. This is basic assertiveness as opposed to aggression or passive acceptance of whatever life offers. But with deep self-love and self-respect, when we don't always get what we want we don't feel too rejected or humiliated. At least we have asked clearly. We keep our dignity in all situations, even while letting go and playing or making fools of ourselves. For we know what our boundaries and limits are and will react appropriately if anyone steps over the mark.

It can also be helpful to improve one's body posture and be aware of holding one's head high, keeping a straight back, and so on. Self-love means that we are telling the world that we *are here*, and that we matter. We can express this in any everyday situation, but it helps to be especially aware of it when walking down the street or in threatening social situations. You can quietly tell yourself that you are important, or even imagine yourself getting bigger and bigger, while a threatening person could be imagined as getting smaller.

Finally, back to Oshun and the dance. Any opportunity to express and enjoy one's body is useful, but dancing is one of the best, for it generally includes sexuality, and to be able to say 'Here I am' and 'I'm sexual' is still hard for many people, especially women. At one time, as a feminist, like many others I would go out of my way not to dress up, look attractive, wear make-up. There was so much anger about being seen as a sex object and not being taken seriously that I stopped enjoying my own sexuality. Oshun is a model of a woman who does show off all her sexual assets, but is strong and in control. And while there are real dangers in patriarchy of being hassled or abused, I have found there are usually at least some situations in which as a woman I can feel safe and enjoy 'flaunting my body'. Sometimes 'women only' parties, even for heterosexual women, can be very sexually exciting places to dance and show off. Even in very patriarchal cultures such as Arabic ones there are usually some spaces for this kind of shared pleasure. They are where 'belly dancing' first came from.

Sexuality and Race

In white Western society there is a hidden shadow. In that shadow lies all the most culturally unacceptable aspects of being human, all the so-called 'inferior' functions of the human being, and most especially its sexuality. It is feared and despised, magnified and diminished, shameful and yet infinitely desirable. It is these sets of extreme opposites that make sex so terrifying, so important. And with this splitting goes the other opposite of Western dualism, the mind versus the body. Sexuality is, of course, associated with the body, although in reality, as most 'experts' tell us, sex is just as much about the mind as the body. But for hundreds of years this hierarchy of thinking has put the body lower, much lower than the lofty mind.

And associated with the body, with nature, with dirt and with chaos have been people of darker skins. Darkness itself becomes associated with the night, with evil and with sexuality, and thus becomes unacceptable. Dark skin colour becomes a symbol for sin. Darkest Africa becomes a metaphor for all that is primitive, instinctual and, of course, sexual. It is even today lodged deep in the unconscious of black as well as white people that having a black skin makes someone closer to nature, more sexual, more exotic, exciting, primitive. But while millions of black people are trying to prove how wrong the stereotype is, white society continues to project all its own unexpressed, feared sexuality onto them. Perhaps images of a black intellectual goddess, for example Black Athena, would be appropriate to help change the stereotyping. But black sexual goddesses like Oshun can be useful too, so long as we are aware of the dangers of dehumanizing people into only one side of themselves. Using goddess images as symbols for different energies that we *all* possess means that we can turn to one goddess and then to another as our needs change.

The point about expressive sexuality is that we *all* have that energy available to us. *All* small babies of whatever colour can be seen wriggling with sheer sexual energy all over their bodies. Freud called this the polymorphous perverse phase because pleasure was not located in only one area of the body. If white people were fully in touch with this energy as they grew up they would not need to project it onto black people.

This projection has been a major feature of the history of the last 400 years or so, helped by slavery, in which economics also played a large part. Black men were seen as workers and studs and women as workers and breeders, or even as sexual playthings for the white bosses. Still today there is the association of the black male with phallic power that is both fascinating and threatening to the white males who have lost touch with their own 'deep masculinity'. And black women are supposed to be especially sexually voracious. These images in the unconscious actually directly oppress black people by limiting the work in which they are expected to excel, to, for example, show business and sport. But they also damage both white and black people indirectly. Psychologically they prevent us from feeling fully human and whole, expressing all sides of ourselves. We all need to take back all the projections that we put onto other groups of people and look at the part of *us* that they represent. This is also part of learning to love oneself.

This process of taking back projections does not deny the differences between people or even the fascination many of us have with difference and otherness. Males and females are 'other' to each other. The problem is one of power. Who is doing the defining? Who sees themselves as 'normal'? Who sees people who are different as 'other'? A group does not usually define *itself* as 'other'. In our society it is overwhelmingly white males who define other groups as 'other'. So difference is turned into hierarchy and black is seen as *inferior* to white rather than just different. In a more rhythmic model of society, difference could be celebrated and enjoyed with neither group dominating. Mutual otherness can be very empowering, exciting and even erotic.

Otherness has always played a major part in sexual relationships, but today there is more freedom for more of us to pursue various kinds of unconventional liaisons. These were once simply the prerogative of the artistic, the intellectual, the very rich or the very poor. Most Western cities are now very cosmopolitan and children grow up more familiar with people of other races and backgrounds. Yet there is still the shadow of racism and classism lurking in the background and it is important to look honestly at what is going on unconsciously in mixed relationships. In the following pages I will examine my own personal history, from growing up in Africa to my own 'mixed relationships', having a black child, and the various stages my process has gone through.

Out of Africa ~ A Personal Story

When I was four and my sister was two, my parents took us to live in Southern Sudan, where my father had been given a job as head of a teacher's training college. They were both committed evangelical Christians and the college was church funded. My mother translated part of the Bible into the local language. The African tribal people and the college students lived in traditional style in small villages made up of mud huts, and grew most of their own food, grazed cattle and mostly wore very few clothes. It was a typical anthropologist's heaven.

But for me it was also home. Our house did have a corrugated iron roof and we did have lots of servants. My parents were very involved with Christianizing, teaching and befriending the African people, and I probably felt rather neglected. We weren't supposed to play with the local children, but I vividly remember wishing that I had been born in an African village instead. The mud huts that almost 'grew' out of the earth seemed very comforting and womb-like. Life seemed slow, contented and above all loving. I began to build up in my head a romantic fantasy about African village life. The babies and children all appeared to be so happy. The cold spirituality of my Christian home, in which there was little affection, contrasted dramatically with the everyday, warm and motherly spirituality of the African village. Several times I ran away. Already I sensed that there were other and perhaps better values and ways of living than my own family's. I did not, of course, think at that age about any negative aspects of local life such as disease or sexism.

This kind of romantic idealization can be found today

Figure 14.   Yemaya in Glastonbury, 1986

around a whole variety of native traditions. All truth, all true humanity, all connection with nature is thought to be found in these cultures. And while, of course, there is much to learn, idealizing can be yet another form of stereotyping and making people into inferior 'others'. This is understandable in a lonely six-year-old but not in an intelligent 30-year-old. My attraction to black culture did, however, have roots deep in my earliest memories and emotions.

When my parents moved to Ghana they sent me to an all-African boarding school run along English public-school lines. I was really too shy to cope with being the only white child, who was both envied and despised at a time of anti-colonial consciousness. It was traumatic. At the same time my father was having an affair with one of his African students. Also traumatic.

In Africa I was the inferior 'other' and I looked up to the African girls as having all the power, the beauty, the confidence that I didn't. I think that for a while I actually wanted to be black. And although in my teens it was always white guys that I fell in love with, in my twenties I started having relationships with black men as well. This was at a time when black political consciousness was very strong, the time of the Black Panthers. I felt a lot of guilt simply about being white. I realize that I let these men treat me quite badly, partly because of this guilt and partly because of that liberal bending over backwards to fit in with what I perceived as cultural behaviour, such as unreliability. At the time I think I thought I was simply being 'cool', not allowing my deeper needs for commitment to show.

However, in my late twenties I did eventually settle down with a beautiful Trinidadian musician who helped a lot to ground me. I became part of his extended family, which satisfied a childhood longing to belong to the African 'village'. I also had a daughter with him, who has grown up within the black culture that I could never fully be a part of. Perhaps I lived out my desire to be black through her! For it is no longer a need in me. She was very much a wanted child although many people, including my parents, assumed that she was a 'mistake' and at one stage my father wanted nothing to do with her or my partner, almost denying that they existed.

We stayed together for seven years, mostly quite happily. But I was always aware of the contradictions under the surface. For example, as a middle-class white woman I had a lot more power in society than he did, yet as a feminist I was only too conscious of the sexism that was also present in our relationship. Somehow his 'lower' social status seemed to balance out the male/female inequality. But after a few years the general imbalance became a problem, especially for him, and resentment crept in subtly, poisoning the love we used to have.

Rediscovering the black goddess was a way for me to reconnect with my African experiences and integrate them with my goddess work, without projecting so much onto actual black people. Perhaps the time has come to do more reclaiming and revaluing of the African traditions and teachings. Luisa Teish has done some of this in the United States, especially in her book *Jambalaya*. Deep respect for these so-called 'native' traditions can help play a part in dissolving racism, but there is much more in the way of consciousness raising needed. Rediscovering the black goddesses and the African traditions can also be a great source of comfort and strength to black people living in a white racist society, especially those who reject the over-Christianized forms of black religion. Other people's stories affirm this to be the case.

Sandra was born in Britain, but her parents were both from Jamaica. When they came to Britain they tried very hard to fit in with the white society and pushed their children hard through the education system. But they still had many habits and attitudes that were embedded in their own backgrounds. Sandra rejected these, feeling deep down rather ashamed of her parents. She didn't like their taste in clothes or furnishing, their food or their strictness. When she got a place at college she left home and found herself a white boyfriend, and soon

moved in with him. Sandra was quite political and certainly
not unaware of racism or sexism. Yet she wanted to forget
what she saw as the lower-class background she had come
from.

She became involved in a feminist group, which eventually
led her to goddess spirituality through one of the white
women attending the group. As she began to learn more about
the black goddesses and connect with them personally, Sandra
began to feel a sense of belonging that she hadn't felt before.
She also went into therapy, as her relationship was on the
rocks. There she was able to express all her feelings of shame
and resentment around her family and move on to an
acceptance and pride. Eventually she ended the relationship
with her boyfriend, feeling that he had stereotyped her as an
exotic sex object without realizing it. She found herself a black
boyfriend, with whom she still had difficulties as he was quite
sexist, but Sandra felt that this was an important step in her
own journey.

Alvin and Claudia met through the church. They fell in love
with each other and spent every possible minute together. The
fact that he was black and she was white felt completely
irrelevant. They were a couple in love. The people around
them seemed to have the same attitude. But when they decided
to get married, all hell broke loose. The respective parents
suddenly changed their tune. The excuse was concern about
the children that Alvin and Claudia would have. In the old
ways of thinking people are supposed to fit clearly into one
category or another, to have a fixed identity. Children of
mixed relationships already have at least two identities. But
then all of us potentially have many different identities.

But apart from any questions about their future children,
Alvin and Claudia also had to recognize that we are living still
in a society with rigid labels, prejudices and stereotypes.
People need to combine a realism about how they are seen by
others with a personal flexibility about identity. It is damaging
to black people who deny that they are black and think white,

partly because sooner or later someone is going to react to them as black, and it is the same in mixed relationships: denial is unhealthy. We all exist on many levels and it could be said that our souls are colourless, and probably genderless too, so when people connect on those levels, colour really doesn't matter. But on a social and political level it does unfortunately still matter. Like sexism, racism is one of the deepest hierarchies in society and until we all learn to think and live non-hierarchically there are very real social *and* economic imbalances that cannot be ignored, just because we prefer to live on that 'other level'.

Alvin and Claudia found a new group of friends who helped them to explore the realities of the social levels of racist reality. They also began to realize how much subtle racism they had actually been experiencing in the church, so left it and joined a pagan group that revered the black goddess. They did eventually marry and have a child, but with much more awareness than would have originally been the case.

Racism is one of the greatest dangers facing the planet at the moment. While economic and political changes are vital, there also needs to be basic changes in our thinking, from hierarchies of superior and inferior, rigid identities and fear, to rhythmic models that celebrate differences, value them equally and allow flexible identities and love. To help with these transitions we need images and myths to give them deep inner meaning. Goddess spirituality does not involve hierarchies. The goddess values everyone equally, not only on the level of soul and spirit, but in the flesh too. Images of the black goddess can be especially useful in the present times of change.

6

Demeter and Persephone

INITIATION RITES

Passages from one phase of life to the next essentially involve a redirection of love energy, or what Freud called the libido. Freud understood this refocusing of energy at different stages of life as changing the emphasis from one part of the body to another, for example from the mouth in the oral stage when one to two years old, to the genitals in the stage of puberty. But we could also see that different kinds of love energy are prominent at different times, and that these may be focused outwards or inwards and onto a particular life task or type of relationship at different stages. Freud had a rather linear, one-directional model, with the so-called 'genital' stage reached after puberty as a kind of final destination of this energy, preferably then contained in a marriage-type relationship. His is simply an energy-based variant on the old 'living happily ever after' myth.

Today we can be more sophisticated about energies and the stages of life. There is more variation and more choice now, so that stages of development and change less often follow expected patterns. A spiral-shaped model would be helpful to chart the changes and the places in our lives to which we may return again and again. At one level all our rites of passage are about love for the mother or mother substitute or desire to return to the womb, and the need to withdraw love from her or it and redirect it into the outside world. There is a constant tension between the longing to merge, and lose the self or the ego, and the need to emerge and stand separate with our love energy directed at will, under our control, into life tasks such as work. Freud called this redirection of libido 'sublimation', almost a kind of second best for what we really want to do with our love, which is to merge with our mothers or go back to the womb. In life most of us keep returning to a symbolic mother and the need to separate from her time and time again. She could be the literal mother that we need to distance ourselves from emotionally, or it could be mother in the form of a sexual partner or an organization that has made us feel safe and secure. Or it could be our home or our country. A rite of passage could therefore be moving house, leaving home, going travelling or even going to live in another country. Rites of passage help us to face that timeless contradiction of the human condition, our need for closeness and our need for separation.

At times in life there is the urge for separation, leading us on to quest for something new. Yet so often, as in the search for the Holy Grail, what we seek is actually to come home to merge once again with 'the divine mother' or her symbol — the vessel, the cup, the womb. All Odysseus's wanderings were in the end to bring him home to the place from which he had come, to home, to Penelope, his waiting wife (mother figure). Yet each time we come home we are different and see it differently from a different point of the spiral. And after the transitional period of change there may be a period of rest or consolidation of the new circumstances, such as being married or being in a new job. Or it may be that the change was from security to insecurity and the next phase is a quest or exploration of some underdeveloped side of one's life. After a divorce, for example, there may be several years of exploring one's sexuality and emotional needs, having various kinds of relationships before settling down to a new state of marriage or a comfortable single life.

Rites of passage or times of transition generally release

enormous amounts of energy, which are needed to propel a person from one kind of life to another. In most cultures of the world in the past, times like puberty have been ritualized in very specific ways. Often there have been elaborate initiation rites involving separation from the mother and even the whole society, going off to special places to receive teachings, to face danger and various tests, even suffering pain through acts like circumcision. Then the initiates are returned to society, but as new people, with new roles, new identities, now able to redirect their love energies towards potential sexual partners and towards contributing as adults to the society.

In modern Western culture there are few clearly defined rites of passage, except in some specific communities such as the Jewish ones, who have their Bar Mitzvah, which is significantly only for boys, at puberty. Confirmation into the Catholic Church can also be a coming-of-age ritual for many. But the actual physical events of a girl's first period or a boy's first wet dream or facial hair are rarely celebrated, and indeed girls are still made to feel embarrassed rather than proud of having their first period.

There are, however, a number of secular events that people consciously or unconsciously use as rites of passage, such as passing the driving test. Losing one's virginity can be another. After all that intense sexual feeling in the teens, the act itself may be more symbolic than anything, a way of acknowledging to oneself and to the world that all this energy does have a purpose. Pouring it into an act of making love focuses that love energy and at the same time shows that one is grown up. There may have been times in the past when such an act was socially ritualized, before a woman's virginity became the property of her husband. Ritualizing a natural act does help concentrate this energy. For so many the feeling one has in adolescence, of something terribly exciting about to happen, is all too often disappointed. The first sexual experience may be a real anti-climax. If it was planned, ritualized and seen as a rite of passage it would more likely have a constructive role in the transition from child to adult that we call adolescence.

Other teenage rituals can include the first job, going away to college, leaving home, wearing particular clothes or visiting particular places (such as clubs). The details would be different for each sub-group. But they can constitute vital rites of passage, with enormous intensities of energy invested in the special event. Then there may be individual rituals that are especially important for one girl or boy but would have no meaning for others, like throwing away a particular teddy bear, cardigan or book. Often transitions involve letting something go, or losing something as well as gaining something else. We talk about *losing* virginity, although it can also be seen as a step into adulthood.

Increasingly today many mothers are encouraging their daughters to celebrate their first menstruation with a party, a gift or a ritual. A ritual I heard about that I thought sounded very powerful was one that took place on a beach. The mother tied a thread from her body to her daughter's and they ran along the beach together; then, when the mother felt tired, they cut the thread together and the daughter went running off ahead. This was a strong symbol of the need to break ties with the mother at puberty. Sometimes this can happen without planning, as many modern individual rituals do. The first time that a girl starts having secrets from a mother who she was really close to could be seen as her way of creating her own rituals for separation. Often, adolescents seem to know instinctively when they need to separate from parents. It is often the parents who find it harder to let go. A mother might feel hurt that her child no longer tells her everything, instead of recognizing it as a transition ritual. The embarrassment that some teenagers feel at being seen in public with their parents can be part of this process too. Rebellious acts such as drug-taking, staying out late, or even illnesses like anorexia nervosa can be seen as desperate attempts to create separation rituals and to become less dependent on parents. They can seem extreme, since the period of transition appears to get longer and longer in Western cultures.

Puberty is not the only time of major transition. Before that there are often other dramatic changes, for example from being a young child dependent on mother to being an older, more independent child. Sometimes this happens around the age of seven, when some children get sent to boarding school or move up to a larger school with older children, or it might be the time that mum first goes out to work. Again there may be individual personal rituals associated with new clothes, such as wearing long trousers for the first time or getting a special pair of trainers. These can represent putting the love energy into caring about the outside world, being loved and admired by peers as well as, or even instead of, your mum. What distinguishes a rite of passage from other life events is often simply the amount of energy invested in it. And it might be different kinds of energy at different stages. For example, at around seven there is a transformation of the love energy from the pull towards mother, safety and being comforted. This energy becomes directed outwards towards developing peer relationships, towards using the body, for example in sport or dance, and towards developing the mind.

This separation from the mother can be traumatic, and may at times seem rather too brutal an initiation. Being sent away to boarding school, for example, has affected thousands of people through into adult life. In some instances a dramatic event may be necessary in order fully to shift the energy that needs to be redirected. It is as if people need to cross a great abyss from one phase of life to another, and in order for them to make the jump they need almost superhuman powers. A traumatic event can give the transition this extra force needed. But not everyone makes it. Some are too damaged by the trauma to continue to the other side and are caught perpetually in the middle, hovering over the abyss, not really 'here'. And if the transition is not forceful enough a person may never change deeply and remain for the rest of their lives essentially a child. Gentler forms of trauma than being sent away to boarding school might include going to a summer camp away from the parents.

At adolescence, and indeed at other times in life, falling in love or becoming obsessed with a hobby, an idea or a person can provide a mild trauma to intensify and focus large amounts of love energy. The transition from single person to married person, for example, is a big change of direction for love energy and needs the trauma of intensification and channelling, through the wedding ceremony, for the leap to be made. Other transitions may not involve a romantic attachment to the one and only person who can 'make your life complete', but rather simply a focus of love energy at a time when you need to change from one phase of life to another. Indeed the person who is the focus of that energy may not even be a person who is going to share the next phase of life with you. Teenagers, for example, often fall in love with unavailable pop stars, or 'get religion' and fall in love with Jesus.

Another feature of these times of transition is that the amount of energy moving around can be so great that the person gets quite exhausted. With the massive hormonal changes happening at adolescence, for example, there often comes an apparent extreme laziness. We all hear complaints about the teenagers who stay in bed all day or go into lengthy sulks. Maybe instead of seeing this as abnormal we could see it as a necessary rest period to help contain the changes. Extra sleep and dreaming may also be necessary to help come to terms with the new role, status or direction of energy.

Adolescence is often experienced as a time of high excitement, a time for exploring, finding out who we are. It may feel like a time when so many choices are available to us. But in order to choose one out of the many, one job rather than others, one school subject above others, one sexual partner above others, we need to let go of all the other possibilities. This can feel like a terrible loss. And such losses need to be mourned; people need to be allowed to feel sad at the losses as well as happy about the gains.

All transition involves loss as well as gain. Losing the security of being a baby in the womb may be the first loss. Then we go on separating from mother in other ways. The first day at school may be exciting, but it includes losing some connection with her. Later on there may be the loss of childhood illusions, such as the idea that our parents are perfect or all powerful. That can be very transforming. Or we may have to lose the idea that we could be top of the class if we really tried. Another kind of painful loss is when that first love affair ends or turns sour. We may have to let go of romantic notions of love lasting for ever, at least in the form in which it is first experienced, which is usually essentially very sexual.

In fact, life can be a constant letting go of illusions. But we often need a trauma such as the break-up of a relationship, or even something as dramatic as an accident or a near-death experience, to completely dissolve deeply held beliefs. Many people are never in their whole lifetimes open to such letting go, and if they never have dramatic events as rites of passage they may never need to look at their belief systems. So in some senses people who have traumatic lives are often forced to grow and change more than those who don't. This may be especially true today, when there are fewer socially organized initiation traumas of the kind that were once forced on everyone.

Therapy as Initiation

Today therapy or growth groups are often used as substitutes for the old initiation rites. People often need help in making sense of the traumatic events that so often mark times of transition. It helps to give them a positive view of what may appear at first to be a totally negative experience, such as a divorce or job loss.

It can also be useful to link the particular event or feelings to the whole of one's journey through life. At times of change it is especially important to understand the past, to understand one's patterns and where they came from in childhood, for example. We can see our lives as journeys that periodically have crossroads when different paths are possible, or when a change of direction is needed. All of life can be seen as a personal myth, set in a personal landscape, with various figures coming in and out to help or challenge us. A problem with a lot of people, women in particular, is that they latch on to someone else's journey, a husband's or child's, or the expected journey of a conventional life, and they never really become the stars of their own lives.

At times of transition especially we may need to have a guide to point out to us what is happening, to help us make our own choices or explore our pasts. This person could be a friend, but it is often more helpful to have an 'objective' outsider whose main purpose is to be a witness to the journey, to give it meaning and importance. A therapist or spiritual teacher might be an appropriate guide during difficult periods. They may be needed only for a few months or a year or so; they can then be returned to later and asked for help if the need arises. They do not need to be a permanent feature of a person's life, with whom a dependency relationship gets built up, although working through a pattern of dependency may be part of what someone needs to do in order to move on to the next phase and further separate from 'mother'. Some people need increased self-esteem in order to have the courage to move on to the next stage. For others it may be most important simply to think differently about their life, to gain new concepts or solve problems. For many people it may be a spiritual transition, involving a major loss of ego and an increased trust of the processes of life or a closer connection with the divine, whatever that means for them. Every transition is different. And a good therapist needs to be able to judge what is most needed for a particular person, rather than having a set theory, technique or belief system that should 'fit' everyone.

Therapy or counselling can be much more flexible than the more rigid steps required in the initiations of specific traditions such as Wicca. Rituals can be tailor-made for the particular individual: for example, burning an object or piece of paper with words on it that represents an aspect of the past that needs to be let go of. Ordinary acts such as giving away old clothes, spring-cleaning or planting a tree can be seen as rituals for rites of passage.

The Eleusinian Mysteries

Although individual, personalized initiations seem to be most appropriate in the modern Western world, we can learn a great deal from the socially organized initiations of ancient mystery religions in which hundreds of people went through the same process at the same time. One of the best known and most influential of these took place in ancient Greece and is known as the Eleusinian Mysteries.

The Eleusinian Mysteries seem to have had very ancient origins, possibly from times before the patriarchal Dorian peoples took over much of Greece. They may well originally have been a puberty rite for girls, possibly combined with an agricultural autumnal or spring festival. But by the time of classical writings on the subject around 600 BC, they had become essentially a massive nine-day-long initiation into the mysteries of Demeter (the corn mother-goddess), in which people experienced a sense of eternal life and became the 'chosen ones' who could die in peace. As details of the rites were secret we cannot know exactly what happened. We do know that anyone who had not 'shed blood' and spoke Greek could attend, including slaves. The mysteries were based around the story of the separation and reunion of the goddess Demeter and her daughter Persephone, providing a sense of the continuity of nature through the female connections. But there were a number of sub-plots, too, and many other dimensions to the mysteries that have fascinated and puzzled scholars for thousands of years.

In the Homeric *Hymn to Demeter* it says that she comes from Crete, where there seems to have been a close connection between nature's changes, for example at springtime, and human transitions, such as puberty. The primacy of nature in the religious beliefs and practices of the Minoans who lived on ancient Crete is described by Lucy Goodison in *Moving Heaven and Earth*. On the island of Thera, once closely connected with Minoan Crete, there are friezes in a special 'house of women's mysteries' which include young girls picking flowers, having a wounded foot bleeding, a goddess or priestess figure and many depictions of spring birds and vegetation. They indicate scenes of female initiation rite with the wound being symbolic of a death, sacrifice or visit to the underworld, or of the first menstruation. The death and rebirth of nature was probably seen as analogous to the death and rebirth required to move to a new phase of life, as at puberty. In these early images there are no men, while in the classical story of Persephone the young girl gets literally carried off to the underworld by a man. Originally she may have had to visit it alone and make her own sacrifice. We can only guess.

Demeter and Persephone

The story starts with the gay and shining young goddess making love in the open on land that had been ploughed three times, with Iachos her lover. This was clearly a ritual act for the fertility of the land, perhaps at the time of sowing. Out of this mating the God Ploutos was conceived, whose name means wealth, and who travels far and wide bestowing riches on everyone he meets. Zeus also lay with Demeter, and with him she had a beautiful daughter who was called Persephone, or sometimes simply Kore (maiden). There was great love and joy between the mother and daughter, and they lived happily together until one fateful day.

Persephone was out in the fields picking flowers with her friends when one particular flower caught her eye. Now unbeknown to her or her mother, Zeus, despite being her father, had agreed to let Hades (or Pluto) of the underworld have his daughter. He had planted a particular flower, the narcissus, to tempt her. For as soon as she picked this flower

Figure 15.   Demeter and Persephone, 1988

a great chasm appeared in the earth beneath her feet and the chariot of Hades came up to take her away. Suddenly she was snatched from the naïvety and gaiety of picking flowers in the sunshine to the dark underworld of Hades. She was raped. She was forced to leave her childhood behind in one swift and brutal act of violence. She was herself the sacrifice. She makes her transition in a state of terror, dragged into the chasm against her will.

Some might argue that it is only through such traumas that deep change can happen. The whole area of sexuality is so frightening as well as fascinating for the adolescent, and girls in patriarchy weren't expected to go exploring themselves. It was only through the act of a man that they could face their own sexuality. But the narcissus flower reminds us of the story of the beautiful youth looking at and falling in love with his own reflection. He was turned into the flower. It is when a young person becomes conscious of their beauty or sexual attractiveness that they become open to the world of adult sexuality. It may be this very self-consciousness that pushes them into making their own descents into the underworld, to do their own sexual and emotional exploring. But this story was written at a time when girls of 13 or 14 were in fact 'sold off' in marriage, often to older men, thus separating them dramatically from their mothers. The old social order where women stayed together and the men moved to their homes had been lost by now. And Demeter's sorrow at the loss of her daughter may also symbolize the loss of that matricentric, female bonding that characterized the older societies.

Demeter roams all over the world seeking her lost daughter, mourning, moaning and sobbing as she goes. In the mysteries the initiates are apparently encouraged to empathize with and feel her suffering, as loss is the first part of any major transition. She refuses to eat and fasting is also often a useful part of any rite of passage. It is both a purifying of the body and an expression of mourning. At first no one would tell her the truth. We start a therapy or initiation process without knowing what to expect; we need to begin sometimes in a state of not knowing. But finally Hecate, who is the wise old woman or crone of the story, told her she had heard the screams of Persephone as she was being raped. Hecate then acts as a kind of support or 'therapist'. She alone was able to hear the terror that everyone else denied. Often a therapist is the first person to whom someone can speak of such experiences without being ignored or invalidated.

Hecate also leads Demeter to find further evidence of the reality of the rape, just as happens in therapy when new light is thrown on past situations. And indeed it was to the sun Helios that they next turned. As Helios sees everything, he too had seen the rape. Now he admitted it. He also suggested that it had taken place with the help of his brother Zeus, who was, of course, also Persephone's father. On hearing this, Demeter became furious, and wandered the earth angrily forbidding plants to grow and animals to thrive. Soon the whole human race was in danger of extinction. This is the extent of the rage that many feel when they re-examine or discover for the first time painful truths about the past. Women today, like Demeter, have allowed that fury to return to consciousness, and it is not just their rage, but that of their mothers and grandmothers before them. It is fury about the male takeover, rape and down-grading of all that is female.

In the end Demeter's powers are so great that Zeus has to beg her to stop destroying the earth. He sends Hermes to tell Hades that he must restore Persephone to her mother or life will come to an end. But he tells Demeter that her daughter can return only if she has not tasted of any of the fruits of the underworld. Hades agreed to send her back; but just as she was mounting the chariot an underground gardener who was standing by began to tease her, saying that he had seen her pick a pomegranate and eat of its seeds. This fruit is red and looks very sexual and womblike. It could represent the idea that once she has tasted of the fruits of adult sexuality she is changed forever, that she can never completely return to the place that she was in before. She has now become the queen of the underworld. She has grown up. She has developed her own underworld powers, the powers of intuition, of listening to the unconscious, of wisdom.

Persephone returns to her mother and they embrace joyfully. This too was no doubt enacted during the Eleusinian mysteries. It could symbolize the return of spring and the continuity of nature, but also the unity of conscious and unconscious, of maturity and youthfulness, an acceptance of the child within us all. But she is now a wise and perceptive child, depicted in most contemporary images as being the same size as her mother. They often seem to be two sides of the same being, sometimes a dark and a light side.

However, the story is not yet over. When Demeter hears about the eating of the pomegranate seeds in the underworld she knows that all is not well. She says that if Persephone must return to the underworld she will not restore the fertility of the land. So Zeus brings in Rhea, the grandmother of all the goddesses and gods, to plead with her. The name Rhea means flow and, coming from Crete, she represents an earlier time when everything in nature may have been seen to flow, rather like the Taoist philosophy of nature. It is no coincidence that it is through Rhea that the dilemma is solved. The solution that everyone finally agrees to is that Persephone will spend two thirds of the year with her mother above ground but will descend to the underworld to be with Hades for the remaining third.

So the solution, as so often in life, is actually to follow a rhythm, to alternate, to recognize that 'either/or' ways of thinking are not the only ones. People can have both, they can express opposite sides of themselves, but at different times. This is often one outcome of therapy. People learn to accept and even appreciate sides of themselves that they did not like before. They may see, as Persephone did eventually, that there are riches too in the underworld. The unconscious has its own wisdom. For women, sex and life with a partner can be a valuable part of life, but does not have to be the whole of life. Time with other women is important too. In fact this division of time can be a useful model for modern heterosexual women who want men or a man in their life, but also want to give time and energy to women, friends, mothers and daughters. Still the primary bond as it mirrors the continuity of nature is between mother and daughter, life proceeding from womb to womb through eternity.

At the same time that Persephone returned a baby was born. Some believe a sacred marriage between Persephone and Hades took place before she reappeared. There may have been a spiritual wisdom here about the paradox of life in death, creation coming out of destruction, links between sex and death, or simply that life goes on eternally with each death being also a rebirth.

I would guess that, as in many religions, the Eleusinian mysteries could be received on many levels by the participants. Those who were ready could see the deeper meanings, while others enjoyed a good pageant and an exciting vision of life after death. Some may have seen the story as symbolizing the planting of seeds in the earth and their eventual sprouting in spring, itself a pretty mysterious event, while others may have seen it as preserving the mother/daughter bond that was in reality usually broken in ancient Greece when the daughter married. But for the psychology of women I like the interpretation that focuses on the daughter cutting ties to the mother, doing her own inner work of separating by visiting her own underworld of the unconscious of sexuality and fear, and then returning a more whole person to reconnect with her mother on more equal, adult terms. This is a pattern that many modern women need to follow. We are all too often still tied to our mothers, either by too much closeness or by rebellion against her. Both approaches keep us stuck. Mothers too need to let their daughters go and may even have to make journeys themselves to force the necessary separation, as I did myself.

When my daughter was 12 I left her with cousins, for the first time, to travel alone to Athens in February to meet my Greek lover and to explore the Eleusinian mysteries. It turned out to be exactly the time of the Greek spring festival, when people prance around the streets in masks and fancy dress, spraying each other with paint, shouting, singing and generally being rather wild. I had arrived at the time of modern spring rites, at the same time of year as the so-called Lesser Eleusinian mysteries. There was a Dionysian madness in the air. We stayed right under the Acropolis, close to the Furies' cave, which gaped, blood red, above us. This was where the Furies were supposed to have fled when Athena judged against them, in favour of the patriarchy. It felt like the entrance to the underworld.

I had cut off from my daughter to re-explore my own sexuality in a mythic manner and for five days felt ecstatic, with only occasional twinges of guilt. Massive doses of hormone, libido, love, whatever you want to call it, were being transferred from my daughter back to men and sex. This felt necessary as we had become almost too close and needed to start further separation. I also had a desire to unravel the mysteries for me personally. What had they to teach me now on my life journey? In a way there was a certain dying within the ecstasy as I gave up all control and let things flow completely for those few days. We rode the 20 miles from Athens to Eleusis (Elefesina) on a crowded bus, not much like the ancient procession. It was very sunny and deserted when we arrived. Pluto's cave did not look at all frightening. It was hard to imagine the torchlight dramas, but we had our own!

By the time I returned to London I felt quite deeply changed after an openness to the full range of intense fear, intense excitement and intense love. I had somehow been initiated. I had at last let go of the tight control over my life and my daughter, the obsession with getting her to school on time, with having the right clothes, the right food, homework done perfectly. Something had to shift in me before she could be more free. From the day of my return the next stage of separation began. She started getting her own books ready for school! I still kept an eye on everything, but felt less of the urgency to be in control that I used to feel. As a single parent the need to control had seemed especially important, since there was no one else but me to keep everything together. Now

I felt I could take more risks, be a bit more selfish and take my own needs more into consideration.

Demeter as the Goddess of Single Mothers

When talking to men, especially in groups, I am constantly amazed at how deeply threatened many of them seem to be by single mothers. This increasingly common phenomenon appears to indicate that men are not needed any more. It is a massive social change that is shaking the very foundations of patriarchal society. Yet most women do not see it in this light. Instead of seeing ourselves at the forefront of social revolution we see ourselves as second class citizens, struggling, often on low incomes, and generally hoping that some man will come along and rescue us. While the economic realities are serious and should not be underestimated, the self-critical state of mind that society encourages us to have can be even more damaging. We are taught to look at ourselves as failures. Yet the strong reactions of men to the whole concept of single mothering imply that actually we are far more powerful and influential than we usually feel. When there is an extreme reaction to a social event or phenomenon it is usually an indication of just how deeply important it actually is. Perhaps the message men are getting is that they are indeed no longer so essential, so desperately needed if they cannot treat women as respected equals. Women can survive without them. But this does not mean that they are not needed at all. Most of us need loving, intimate relationships, and for the majority of women these are sought with men.

During a workshop I led for single mothers it became clear that there was a deep need for encouragement, positive thinking and support, as well as for sharing practical problems and solutions. As I was using goddess imagery in other areas of work I began to explore goddesses as single parents. In many of the oldest stories and oldest societies there seems to have been an emphasis on the mother/child (later specifically mother/son) relationship, with the man as rather peripheral. Even the word 'husband' meant a man who came to the woman's home to look after *her* property and work on *her* land. He was often seen as the 'stranger', even in early Greece where Zeus, the ultimate man's god, was originally the god of strangers.

This ownership of land and the centrality of the female role in the family must often have made women feel as powerful as men in those societies. But they did still have men in their lives as lovers and husbands. The main difference was that they were not too economically dependent and were freer to get rid of partners who did not satisfy them. The central relationship may more often have been between mother and children. This alone was a blood relationship, rooted in the continuity of human flesh as part of nature. This connection was what patriarchy eventually succeeded in breaking, putting the emphasis instead on the man as head of the family, owning wives and children, and placing the male/female relationship far above the female/child relationship.

The present increase in the number of families headed by a single mother could be seen as a way of unconsciously returning to the older, more 'natural' kind of social system, only in a modern way. For we cannot actually 'go back'. But it may be a vital part of a movement away from crumbling patriarchy to a more interconnected, co-operative way of living. At present the economic system forces millions of single-parent families on to the breadline, and many are unsupported by either society or friends, leaving children insecure and angry. But there is no god-given rule that children are better off in nuclear families than in other kinds of families. In many parts of the world and for many thousands of years before the industrial revolution created the nuclear family, children were brought up with a whole variety of arrangements. What makes it hard today for children is the powerful myth presented by the media, the church and even schools, that the nuclear family is superior to other kinds. Any strong social norm has a deep effect on the psyche of the population, but is not biologically given. Indeed if biology was all that mattered the single mother would be seen as 'natural'. And economic deprivation in any kind of family also has a damaging effect on children. It is the preservation of patriarchy at all costs that motivates society either to ignore or oppress the reality of single parenting, especially single mothering. The recent spate of movies about the importance of fathers can be seen as part of this desperate attempt to stem the tide of social change.

Patriarchal religions play a vital part in upholding the rights of the father and denigrating single mothers, especially if they have become pregnant outside marriage in the first place, worst of all if they have actually chosen to be single mothers. The most poisonous venom is saved for those mothers who don't even want a man to be around. Women who have never had sex with a man but want a child through artificial insemination have been seen as the most evil women of all. Why? They threaten patriarchy at its most fundamental level. This is all despite the fact that the Virgin Mary was supposed to have had Jesus without having sex with a man!

New religious mythology is needed to counteract the still profound impact of Christianity and other male-dominated religions. Demeter is for me the goddess who most clearly embodies the values of single mothers. She was the centre of the Eleusinian mysteries, and so played an important role in the religion of ancient Greece, even as it became increasingly patriarchal. But she was probably originally an Earth-mother goddess of the cycles of nature, so in a sense she was as powerful as the gods of patriarchal religion. Even in the Homeric story in 600 BC she has the capacity to destroy the fertility of the earth. Her role as supreme mother is her main one, and as she takes on more human characteristics in the story it turns out that on that level too her main focus is on her daughter. She does have lovers, including the great Zeus, but her daughter is far more important to her than they are. When she discovers that Zeus has played a part in Hades' abduction of Persephone, she is absolutely furious with him.

Contrast this attitude with the way that so many modern women stick by their men even when they know that they have been abusing their own children.

Demeter also has a carefree and sexual side as expressed in her making love in the thrice-ploughed field. And although she did not have a husband she was the goddess who initiated couples into the joys of lovemaking. This is a fact about Demeter that is often forgotten. Patriarchal society finds it hard to reconcile motherhood with sexuality. The Virgin Mary is seen as completely asexual. Imagine what different attitudes we would have if our main deity was a beautiful, sexual, single mother instead of a stern father figure!

Ann had been married to Mark for 14 years and had two children now aged 10 and 13. They had not been getting on for many years, but Ann was afraid to leave because she was dependent on him financially and they had built up a very comfortable life together. Then she met Peter, who was totally different from any of her friends. He was a jazz musician recently separated from his wife and living in a rather scruffy bedsit, trying to write a novel and doing session work to pay the bills. His daughter went to the same school as Ann's son and there was an instant attraction between them. Eventually he invited Ann to come and hear him play at a local pub. Ann was terrified of walking into pubs alone. She tended to live her social life with her husband or with her one special woman friend. She never did anything on her own. So this event was in itself a kind of initiation into a new stage of life. She managed to arrive at the pub, nervous but somehow driven by something that was beginning to feel uncontrollable. The inevitable happened, they ended up back at his place and embarked on an affair. Ann fell madly in love. Peter was enthusiastic at first, but, as was his pattern, once the first flush of romance was over he moved on to seek greener pastures. Ann clung on for months. Eventually she went into therapy and realized that the affair was actually telling her something about her own life. She needed to change.

Figure 16. Reaching for the Moon, 1985

Soon after the affair finished Ann decided to find a job, and began a process of transformation that led to her leaving home and finding a flat of her own. She kept the children with her and it really was a financial struggle. But the worst aspect of it was the way that old friends shunned her. She was no longer invited to their dinner parties. As a single woman she was suspect, perhaps reminding others of a freedom they didn't have, or perhaps a threat because of her availability. Did they think she was after their husbands? Her best friend did remain loyal and soon Ann joined an evening class on women and mythology where she met more independent-minded women, some of whom became friends. She also learnt about the ancient stories of goddesses and their consorts and the pre-patriarchal importance of the mother/child bond as opposed to the mother/father one. These ideas and the support she was getting gave Ann a great deal of strength. Although she felt bitter sometimes about the jazz musician, she realized that the affair had been a vital concentrating of energy to help her make that leap across the abyss from settled housewife to independent woman.

Lucy was terrified of growing up. She was nearly 18 but looked much younger and didn't eat much. She was always on a diet, having to be in control of this frightening body that kept threatening to blossom into a woman. Her parents had split up when she was 10 and her mother had never remarried but was a dedicated career woman. Lucy had never been interested in boys and was still deeply angry, in her unconscious, about her father leaving. In therapy she was able to get in touch with and express some of that anger and also talk about her feelings towards her mother. Lucy had unconsciously felt that she must protect her mother, so was not daring to have relationships in case they took her away from her. Eventually she began to see that she needed to separate from her mother and had her own life to lead. Her mother was a strict Catholic and Lucy's first rebellion was to leave the Catholic Church and become a Pagan. In her explorations of the goddess in paganism she found that there could be archetypal mother figures who could comfort and support her as replacements for her own mother. She related more and more to these figures, some of whom were strangely like the Virgin Mary. She also saw many different models of 'grown-up' people who were not like her mother and became less afraid of growing up. Once she had met a young man and started having sex with him, all her diet obsession disappeared and she no longer feared her body.

Sam was a very shy boy who was also terrified of growing up. His father was a very macho man, a policeman who ruled the household through fear. Everyone knew that he had a terrible temper and almost tiptoed around him just in case he lost control. Sam learnt to control himself extremely well, and repressed not only his own anger at his parents but also his sexuality. Yet by the time he was 19 sexual fantasies kept popping into his mind and he became obsessed with one girl after another. He was, however, so determined not to be like his father that he didn't really want to be a man at all. When Sam went into therapy he was able to recognize and express all the bottled-up feelings and he decided to move away from home. He then found himself a spiritual teacher and became completely devoted to her and the teachings of her group. This obsession with the spiritual teacher was needed to help him make a transition into adulthood. Around her he also met a whole variety of different kinds of men who were not like his father; many were quite feminine and sensitive. He was able to allow himself to become the kind of man he wanted to be, rather than the kind prescribed by society. He also found himself a girlfriend who began to balance out his obsession with the teacher. His energies became more diffuse and more easily channelled into whatever he chose.

Most people do find a way to separate from their parents and grow up. It is, in fact, often the ones who question what being adult means and rebel against being like their parents who have the most rewarding journeys in the long term. We all need to question what being adult means today. What are the possibilities? We don't have to stay stuck in the limited identities that society has carved out for us.

7

The Dionysian Mysteries

RITES OF PASSAGE

Love energy as an ecstatic force seems to have been consciously used in ancient rites of passage such as the Dionysian mysteries in ways that contain, transform and redirect it. Yet in modern societies it is largely repressed, only to burst out in extreme forms such as mass hysteria, easily manipulated by right-wing groups such as the Nazis. Like everything else in nature, this energy has its natural rhythm when it is given space for genuine expression. There needs to be a balance in any society between what are sometimes called the Dionysian energies of letting go and ecstasy, and the containing energies of control and holding. Where this balance has been lost and there is a one-sided emphasis on control, the Dionysian energies tend to erupt dangerously. In an individual we can also find such blind eruptions, as when an over-controlled person suddenly gets very drunk or runs off with his or her secretary. Such outbursts can be destructive when they are purely unconscious reactions. We have lost the hidden wisdom of ancient societies who consciously incorporated loss of control into their social structure. Perhaps there are remnants of this wisdom in the cyclical religions, such as Catholicism, with their festivals, carnivals and so on, still enjoyed in many parts of the world.

Today it may be that, as we live in a very individualistic

Figure 17. Earth Mysteries, 1983

culture, we each have to find our own ways of rediscovering the right balance for us and of using these energies in a constructive way. Unfortunately even therapists are often afraid of the power of these energies and people who fully express them can be labelled mad, manic or even simply bad. The Freudian model implies that the healthy person should sublimate such energy at all times and it has little sense of cyclical life or of very different life phases once adulthood has been reached. Becoming a responsible citizen implies leaving behind such childish or adolescent behaviours as Dionysus would encourage.

Dionysus

Much has been written about Dionysus, but here I want to stress the aspects of him that are relevant to women and men in times of transition, in times when relations between the sexes are in a state of flux. The stories of his birth vary, but the best known involves him being born twice. Zeus disguised himself as a mortal and had a secret love affair with Semele, who was a moon priestess. She became pregnant with Dionysus, but after six months asked Zeus to show his true self, on the advice of his jealous wife, Hera. Zeus obliged by turning himself into a flash of lightning and thunder, which is the natural force he originally represented. An ordinary woman could not survive such a direct encounter with lightning, so Semele was immediately burnt up. But Hermes saved the child; he opened up the thigh of Zeus as a second womb, put the baby (foetus) inside and sewed it up. While on one level this could be seen as yet another patriarchal attempt to deny the importance of birth from a woman's body, it also has a more profound meaning akin to the Christian idea of needing to be born again in order to reach a full relationship with the divine. Yet after he was born Dionysus spent his life searching for the mother that he had lost, as so many men do today, looking for their mothers in every woman they love.

Dionysus therefore has both divine attributes and very earthy, human needs. He never forgets the real mother in whose womb he began to live. He is indeed the god of opposites, sometimes called 'the child of the double door'. He belongs to both men and women. The bisexual nature of this god is amplified in the next part of the story.

The baby boy, who had horns and was crowned with serpents, was once again the target of Hera's jealousy. She ordered the Titans, who were the gods and goddesses of older times, to tear him into shreds. This they did, no doubt with great enthusiasm. But they knew the old ways and all about death before transformation and rebirth. So they boiled all the pieces in a cauldron, and with the help of his grandmother Rhea, who represents the flow between opposites, he came back to life.

The cauldron of transformation is a vital symbol in all ancient goddess-orientated cultures. Indeed, therapy can be seen as providing the cauldron of containment and magical inner space in which the person who has dared to let themselves break down into little pieces can be put back together again. For with no separating into parts there can be no reuniting of them in a more integrated and conscious way. In therapy we try to understand all the parts of ourselves, including the initially unacceptable ones. When we have analyzed and broken down all the parts, only then can we put them together, but in a different relationship. Initially, for most of us, the parts are first joined unconsciously by hierarchical structures that imply one part, such as reason or cheerfulness, is superior to another side, such as emotion or sadness. We have to separate the opposites before we can reunite them rhythmically as both being equally valuable. If we can trust grandmother Rhea through the process of therapy, we will be reintegrated eventually.

Dionysus was then given to Persephone, who in some stories is also his mother, as he has strong underworld connections. She was supposed to have conceived him by making love with Zeus when he was disguised as a serpent.

This may well be an even older story, as the serpent was indeed the first consort of the goddess when she was more powerful. Persephone gave Dionysus to a king and persuaded him to bring up the child in the women's quarters disguised as a girl, so that Hera would not find him again. Dionysus was very much a god of women. He was familiar with women and had a strong womanly aspect himself. In many ways he seems to have been the kind of male energy that women ideally create for themselves if given the chance. He was always in the company of women, such as his wild Maenads, and yet he is the only Olympian god who remained faithful to his wife, Ariadne.

Hera was not, however, so easily fooled and punished the king and his queen by sending them mad. Hermes again intervened and changed him first into a kid, then into other forms, to avoid capture. Dionysus is the god of change and is known for his many transformations, which can be an example to us of the many different sides that we all have, the different subpersonalities. Change is a part of life, and while for some too much changeability could imply madness, perhaps it is those who are stuck in only one side of themselves who are really the sick ones.

Eventually Hera accepted Dionysus as Zeus's son, so he was able to acknowledge his father, which is an important part of anyone's therapy process. Yet he was still seeking his lost mother, Semele. He wandered all over the world with his band of wild women, having many adventures. Then eventually he came to the island of Naxos, where Ariadne had just been abandoned by her mortal lover, Theseus. She was in despair over her lost man, Dionysus was in despair over his lost mother. In the depths of their pain they came together and created a divine union, of the human and the spiritual, suffering and bliss, chaos and new order.

The marriage of Dionysus and Ariadne was at the centre of the Dionysian mysteries and seems to be a representation of the essence of paradox that lies at the heart of most mysteries. In death or near death came love, rebirth, bliss. In some stories

Ariadne does also literally give birth. At the very moment of greatest despair, when reaching the bottom of that dark hole of depression, can come new light, a new hope, a new kind of marriage, not to a human mortal but to the divine lover, to the divine energy that is our birthright. We may not reach this point until we have experienced despair either through loss or by trying all the human earthly pleasures and goals, pushing to the limits all that we are taught to want in ordinary life. At the point of realization that none of this can fully satisfy, we 'fall in love' with god(dess) instead. For men perhaps it involves giving up the search for the perfect mother and for women letting go of the romantic hero image.

Dionysus was called the loosener, the shaker, the liberator, and he helps in the dissolution of old structures and conventions. He is vitally needed in any time of great social or individual change. His energies come from the underworld, from the unconscious and from the primal rhythms of nature. But Western culture today does not trust them. They are seen as being totally out of control. Only if we have a rhythm model of life rather than a hierarchical, control model can we appreciate the order that actually flows within nature, within the instincts, within chaos.

It is often an important part of people's inner journeys to descend fully and wholeheartedly to the instinctual world of Dionysus. Therapy in its many forms may help and encourage such a descent, but all too often people try to do it for themselves, unconscious of the fact that they are actually reaching out for an essential human experience. They may use drugs or alcohol or 'falling in love' to achieve this necessary total letting go. But then society will usually condemn them, repress them and drive them into the very addiction that is feared. If the method by which ecstasy is reached is seen as bad, it is all the more likely that a person will be ashamed and so become obsessed. This obsession all too often leads to the kind of secretive addiction, such as alcoholism, that we all know about.

If ecstasy was not seen as shameful and was an ordinary part of everyday life, private obsession would be less necessary. Indeed, in cultures where drugs are taken very occasionally as part of a sacred ritual, addiction is less common. In the same way it seems likely that in those ancient cultures in which sexual ecstasy was seen as sacred and an occasional but normal part of life's rhythms, there would probably have been less in the way of addictive relationships, love obsessions, sex addiction, and so on, that we are hearing so much about today.

The implication in a lot of the literature on addictions is that the recovering, non-addictive or 'healthy' person has no more need of ecstasy. Life should be lived at a calmer and more gentle pace, even seeming bland at times, getting on with social achievements and obligations. Again there is little sense of needing different approaches to life at different times and stages of growth. Nor is there much sense of using ecstatic experiences consciously and specifically to enable a passage from one stage to another. In the rhythmic model of life the 'healthy' person has times both of control and of letting go, and neither is seen as better than the other. The important issue is the intuitive sense of when it is appropriate to be in one mode or the other. It is also important to learn to contact and enjoy one's *own* ecstatic feelings, enthusiasm and joy, without depending on another person or a substance to provide them.

Ecstasy can be transformed at certain times of life from an intense, specific experience into a more general sense of well-being and into the ecstasy of everyday life. This may be especially important at times of transition when society tells us we are having to leave behind youthful pleasures, when it may be implied that only the young and irresponsible can experience ecstasy.

The word 'ecstasy' in Greek actually means being 'beside oneself'. It can be an experience of being part of something greater than oneself, something external, something overwhelmingly beautiful and powerful. But this energy can be brought back into the self, grounded and turned into a more loving way of being in ordinary life, while doing the washing-up or waiting at a bus-stop. This kind of love does not have to be triggered by another person or external stimulus but comes from the inside, to be directed at will towards anything or anyone. Transforming the ecstasy is therefore not a loss of joy or youth or fun, but a gain of more permanent love. If this aim were consciously understood, people would not need so much to lose themselves in ecstatic experiences. They would be better able to use the enormous amount of energy that becomes available at such times to contact their deepest selves, understand themselves better and live more fully in everyday life.

The Dionysian Mysteries

This process of going deep into the instincts and then coming back 'up' to reintegrate them into a more whole self has been called individuation by Jungian analysts. And some of them, Linda Fierz-David and Nor Hall, for example, have linked the Roman Dionysian mysteries specifically to this process. These are the most recent examples of a mystery religion that probably went back thousands of years to Minoan Crete and before. A depiction of a Dionysian initiation painted on the wall of a Roman villa near Pompeii shows what actually went on in those rites. The meaning of the actions, feelings and symbols expressed there can only be guessed at, but certain features do seem similar to the modern therapy process. Most people come into therapy at times in their lives when they are facing transitions. Therapy can be a safe place away from the world to experience a certain degree of 'madness' or descent into that state of letting go or psychosis that all babies experience to some extent. It involves the two opposites of control and letting go. The therapist keeps the sense of reality and the boundaries, allowing the client to lose hers for a while. In the same way the mysteries are presided over by one or more priestesses who remain calm and contained but are not without empathy. Indeed, it is likely that they will themselves have experienced reaching that primal baby state, the primal

Figure 18.   Ariadne's Mysteries, 1991

wound, the primal scream, the loss of everyday structure, and have come out stronger and wiser. Therapists who have never dared make the descent may not be able to provide the same opportunity for deep change in their clients. Perhaps the best therapists are those who have allowed some 'break down' in their own lives, as Jung himself did in the years leading up to the first World War.

The sequence of events depicted on the wall at Pompeii is as follows. First the initiate arrives with a veil over her head. This could imply a separateness from the everyday world and going to a special, sacred place, as the therapy room can be. A young boy then reads to her from a book. This could be the intellectual framework in which any therapy needs to take place. There are usually some concepts needed by the mind to give a safety and structure to the process of letting go. Simply getting drunk or dancing all night or even falling in love without a mental understanding of why and for what purpose this is happening can be a limited experience at the least and, at worst, a step on the way to potential self-destruction. So the words are important. Throughout this book I describe a framework in which opposites such as control and letting go are seen as rhythmically connected and life is seen in terms of stages, transitions and cycles, with love energy as the connecting principle. This basic set of ideas can give meaning to ecstatic experiences. Stories and myths, either of gods and goddesses or of people's own lives, described at the beginning of an initiation also give the experience meaning.

The next part of the Dionysian initiation appears to involve a gift of cakes or perhaps a sacrifice. Cake, like the bread and wine of Christianity, could represent the body of the sacrified god. As we saw in the story of Dionysus, he was indeed broken into many pieces, only then to be reborn as a new whole. In our personal therapies we too may need to make sacrifices, of money, of time, of illusions about ourselves. I found that sacrificing the image I had of myself as a nice, giving person was difficult in the early days of my therapy. For some people even just coming into therapy is a sacrifice of their image of themselves as someone without problems. Learning to be humble and to submit to the process is vital in this first part of the rites, as it is in therapy. It is also vital that the therapist does not use this stage to impose his or her own power or feel superior in any way. Therapists too need to be humble and trust the goddess or god or process that is present between them and their clients.

It appears that a number of rituals are then performed to prepare the initiate. Water is poured over a laurel leaf, which is then placed in a basket that seems to contain a snake or phallic object. The laurel leaf may have been chewed to help reach an ecstatic state, but it had to be purified first. Any drugs or alcohol taken as part of a controlled ecstatic experience need to be 'blessed' or somehow imbued with sacred meaning, and thus purified, like a glass of wine held up to the light with thanks given to the goddess.

The basket and phallic object inside seem to have played a vital part in many mysteries. The basket was probably associated with the winnowing basket in which corn seeds are sorted out. But it also symbolized the womb or vagina with the penis or phallic energy inside. There are strong sexual connotations, and at this point of the process there is an air of building excitement and anticipation. When in therapy or in life generally something important is about to happen, people often have a sense of almost sexual excitement, without knowing quite why. This is of course especially strong in adolescence, when there is that feeling of something wonderful about to happen, but what?

In the next part of the rite Silenus, Dionysus's old tutor, appears, playing a lyre. And suddenly the scene changes to a natural, rural environment, perhaps symbolizing a return to childhood feelings of oneness with everything. Certainly music can inspire such feelings in people. This stage could be seen as a phase of naïve ecstasy or a symbiotic union with the mother, a merging. This is what people often long for in relationships, in therapy, in life. It is a primitive kind of loss of self, being carried away by the music.

Then suddenly the scene changes again and there is a terrified woman depicted on the wall. At this point there may be a sudden separation or an awakening from that primal bliss. In therapy, perhaps after exploring childhood and seeing the therapist as the safe, good mother, suddenly she goes on holiday or something happens that makes the client have to face her worst fears, for example of abandonment. In the background old Silenus holds up a grotesque mask. This might also be the point where one has to take off the mask of everyday life and face the real self underneath. This usually happens in therapy, but it is also a stage in people's lives, as when the first bliss of naïve love in a relationship changes and the real person behind the projected mask shows her or himself. There may be a descent into an underworld of fear or depression.

Then the initiate returns, having been through some experience such as facing a deep fear, able now to face the phallic object in the basket consciously. The ecstasy is contained. Behind her the figures of Dionysus and Ariadne sit voluptuously, suggesting a contained and contented sexuality. The initiate seems to lift a veil off the phallic object, perhaps really to see it for the first time. This could represent an honest facing of one's own sexuality, or specifically an honouring of phallic energy as sacred and valuable to women as well as men.

Yet this scene is followed by a dark angel appearing with a whip, which could either be an infliction of pain as a mark of initiation, or a sado-masochistic sexual experience, or a form of humiliation that all initiates have to go through in order to submit fully to the divine. There may be a confession of 'sins' here, a going down to one's most shameful side in order to feel shame no more. And certainly in our culture there is still a lot of shame around sexuality.

After this the initiate emerges, naked and dancing. It seems at this point that she is now ecstatic again, but this time in a more conscious and mature way. She is united with the divine. All the energy that she at first merged with, then separated from, then feared, then admitted to having, has now become incorporated into her self. She can dance naked with no shame. She *is* goddess or god, not merely merged with her or him. The pictures end with an ordinary domestic scene in which Cupid holds up a mirror to the woman. Now she really knows herself and can incorporate all that energy into everyday life and love. This final outcome is perhaps the main aim of many therapies: self-knowledge and learning to let that love energy or libido flow freely within the necessary containments. The result is a rhythmic interconnection between the Dionysian energies and the structures of ordinary life.

If these two sides are not brought together, the Dionysian energies can lead to the kind of hysteria that is often associated with times of change such as the menopause. It is believed that the Roman Dionysian rites were in fact especially for mature women moving into their mid-life. This, like any other borderline time, is potentially a moment of danger. Strong emotions are often around. Hormones are changing. There is often heightened sexuality, a lot of rage, a feeling of wanting to scream or run away.

It can also be a time when pleasure is pushed to its extreme, in order perhaps to discover its limits. There may be nothing to lose, no more responsibilities (such as children). It is interesting that women are supposed to reach their sexual peak after 35, and it may be even later, while men are supposed to reach theirs at 19. This is a strange biological mismatch. But there may be all kinds of advantages, for while women are supposed to be looking after children it may not help the survival of the species to have them also being sexually adventurous. Once women are past that stage, they can allow the full range of their sexual potential to flower. And there may be another, even more important factor. As we have already seen in this book, sexual and spiritual energies are very similar. Since all this sexual energy that women often have in their middle life is not needed for producing children, it can be used for something else, perhaps equally vital for the well-being of the species. This energy can be transferred into healing, spiritual energy, and into wisdom. Mid-life could actually be a time to look forward to. Certainly, the Dionysian mysteries can give us some clues as to how such passages may be negotiated meaningfully and constructively.

Stages of Life and Rites of Passage

Two major life transitions that can be understood as rites of passage are young adulthood, when greater responsibilities are being taken on, often experienced around the age of 25 to 30; and the 'mid-life crisis', around age 35 to 56. People do of course experience these rites of passage at different times and in different ways, but there are often seven-year cycles that people can look back on and recognize. Cells in the human body renew themselves every seven years, and there are accepted notions such as the seven-year itch in relationships, or the idea that the age seven is a special turning-point before which most of our personality is laid down. Astrologically, the Saturn return, which occurs when Saturn is at the same point in the sky as it was at a person's birth, happens at around age 28/29 years (i.e. 4×7). This is often a major turning-point in people's lives. But the seven-year-cycle idea does not work for everyone, and in our culture reaching one's 30th or 40th or 50th birthdays may seem more significant.

It is important in the rhythm model of life to recognize that each stage is as vitally important, potentially exciting and transforming as any other. In our society we tend to think of life as going in a straight line up to some fictitious peak, perhaps for men around 40 and for women around 25, and declining from then on! We tend to put youth on a pedestal and see older people as inferior. The hierarchies of ageism are oppressive to everyone, for there is a deep fear of growing old even amongst the young. Instead we need to see each phase as equally valuable, with its own challenges and rewards. This is not to deny or fight against the physical facts of ageing, as those in the beauty business try to, but to value fully each stage. All the rites of passage do involve a loss and a sacrifice as well as a gain. The loss may need to be mourned, but the gain also needs to be joyfully embraced. Ecstatic experience can help with such transitions, in or out of therapy.

A therapist, guide or friend may help a person going through powerful experiences in their everyday life to see the significance of them in terms of passage. The therapy itself may also evoke intense feelings, such as when clients 'fall in love' with their therapist. These feelings too can be understood and contained. I have worked a lot with people going through transitions in their mid to late twenties and early thirties, perhaps as for me this was a very difficult time. At that age I had a very strong desire to have a child, having spent my twenties exploring life, relationships, sex and politics in a rather ungrounded way. But I did not want to give up what I perceived as an exciting life. I believed that there were either the boring, stable, marriage-type relationships and lifestyles, or the adventurous, free liaisons that I had enjoyed till then. I was caught in the middle, very stuck. So I unconsciously made my own ritual. I decided that the truth was not to be found in books, that all my intellectual adventures had their limits and that only love, spiritual love, really mattered. So I gave away every single book that I owned, much to the horror of my friends, and flew off to Canada to see if a boyfriend who lived there was a possible serious relationship. It was a turning-point in my life. The boyfriend turned out to be wrong for me then, but I returned feeling both clearer and a bit more grown-up. About six months later, after buying my own flat, I met a musician who seemed to want some stability too. So I had the exciting life of living with a musician *and* the security of my own home and a solid relationship, which lasted for the magical seven years.

A woman called Sue came to me at a similar age. She was 32 and just could not 'find the right man'. What she said she really wanted was a baby. She had not had a relationship at all for about four years and wondered what was wrong. It became clear through therapy that she, like many other women today, did not really want the restrictions and stereotyped roles of a conventional marriage or partnership, so she was actually highly ambivalent about commitment. She didn't want to give up her freedom. Together we explored the way she too had seen life in terms of either/or, and whether perhaps there were more alternatives available in the middle. She had previously always fallen in love with exciting, mysterious and often unreliable men, while she herself was very sensible and saw herself as a bit dull. The men had played the role of Dionysus for her. She had yet to discover her own 'inner' Dionysus. Much of the work with Sue was helping her to get in touch with the wild side within herself. Gradually she began to let go more, to go dancing regularly, for example. She stayed in bed for longer at weekends and even let herself get a bit drunk a couple of times. Her life began to be more of a rhythm between letting go and control. Of course, we also had to look at where her desperate need to be in control came from, which turned out to be a childhood pattern because her mother had been so out of control. She had had to mother her own mother.

Gradually Sue learnt to 'worship' the god Dionysus, not his embodiment in human men. She finally did a ritual that we worked out together which evolved from a series of paintings of herself as a wild woman, and included dressing up in clothes she would never normally wear and then finally visualizing the god Dionysus coming to her. Her room was prepared for this personal 'marriage': incense was burning, food laid out and favourite music playing. She imagined him in the form she chose herself, visualized him dancing with her and then finally caressing her and making love with her. She was able to bring herself to orgasm eventually and experienced a great rush of energy. After this she was more able to incorporate ecstasy into her life. Soon afterwards she did meet someone to share her own exciting self with, even though he was not as 'exciting' as her previous lovers. She didn't need him to be, as she had her own source of ecstasy. Having a baby became less important to her as her life became more full, although she still might choose to become a mother.

Another rite of passage story comes from a man we'll call

John, a very successful advertising art director, 28 years old, and very attractive. After a teenage romance that hurt him deeply, John had never allowed himself to fall in love again. He had always found it easy to attract women and have lots of sex and fun, but now he saw that most of his friends were settling down into marriages or at least live-in relationships. He had fewer and fewer people to go clubbing with. He too had a horrifying picture of becoming grown up, imagining a mortgage and children and terrible responsibilities. He thought that he could cope with these only if he was 'really in love'. Only that would provide the ecstasy needed to jump across that abyss. Yet another problem was that he had a very specific idea of his perfect woman.

We explored his childhood patterns with a rather cold mother, as well as the social expectations of the culture. Time was also spent mourning the relationship in his teens that had gone wrong. But it also seemed especially important to work with the containment of all that Dionysian energy that he was afraid to lose. He began to stop seeing things so rigidly in terms of either/or choices and more as rhythms between different sides of the self, and endless creative possibilities. We explored his inner feminine, his own personal Ariadne, who helped his hero self through the labyrinth and was then able to 'marry' and earth his Dionysian self. He practised visualizing her meeting him beside the sea-shore and eventually merging with him. He imaged a safe and beautiful place where he could lie down with her, a place he could return to whenever he chose, which helped to allay his desperate need of women, any women. John actually chose to be celibate for a while in order to work on his own inner security. And he also worked out a natural rhythm for himself of leading a controlled, disciplined life and letting go only at weekends. So his Dionysian side was given expression, but in the context of a more ordered life, no longer totally out of his control.

Both Sue and John also spent a lot of time in therapy working out what their real needs were, as opposed to those imposed on them by society, friends or family. Many people seem to reassess their lives at this time, possibly after going up the path given them by others in their teens and twenties. Sometimes events such as loss of a job, getting pregnant or falling in love can force this reassessment process. By seeing adulthood in a less stereotyped way, people can actually look forward to having a future life more in keeping with their real needs, and one that does not need to be devoid of freedom and fun.

If reaching 30 is seen by so many as the beginning of the end, imagine how much worse it can be when reaching mid-life. Here again rites of passage and a more balanced view of the next stage can help people get through the transition.

For me there were clear seven-year patterns. From 28 to 35 I settled down and put most energy into raising my child and creating a home. Then I began to feel a strong urge to improve my career, and from 35 to 42 I went back out into the world, developed my therapeutic and training skills, published my first book, built up a good practice and separated from my partner. A lot of my energy was towards women. Most of my work was with women. I began to set up the Serpent Institute, a feminist therapy training centre. But around the age of 42 my personal and emotional needs, which had been neglected, began to emerge. And for me, the rites of passage were a series of intense sexual and spiritual experiences and eventually falling in love, which rocked my whole being to its core and made me question much of the structure on which I had built my life. I also opened up again to men, which has been interesting as well as painful. It feels as though my rites of passage have been to do with my own personal 'marriage' to Dionysus or Eros or my own spiritual sexual energy, to bring it into my everyday life rather than to focus it on particular men. It has felt like an initiation into love. One of my personal losses has been the idea that men are the enemy and that women should not depend on them at all if possible. I still believe that patriarchy has deeply damaged relations between the sexes and that they may not be fully healed for hundreds of years. But I can see now that some, although definitely not all, of my resistance to men has been to do with my personal background and low expectations around intimate relationships.

Many of my friends and clients are going through one form of mid-life crisis or another. Some examples include Mary, who was married for 20 years to a supportive husband. She devoted most of her energy to bringing up their two sons, and on the surface they were a happy family. But once the youngest son reached 16, she suddenly started going to clubs and flirting in what her husband found a most undignified way with men young enough to be her son. She particularly liked Latin men, who were very charming with her. Eventually she fell in love and had an affair with one of these men and for weeks seemed to be in a daze, forgetting to do any housework. Mary was going through a perfectly reasonable rite of passage in which she was moving from a life phase where her energy went into children and the home to one where it was needed for herself and expressing her full potential, including her sexual side. Interestingly her husband became much more sexually interested in her at this time. She felt more fully alive. The first few frantic months eventually turned into a more rhythmic enjoyment of the Dionysian side of life, with weekly dancing, attending painting classes and a holiday on her own. Luckily, through therapy and an understanding husband, Mary was able to negotiate this transition satisfactorily and was accepted. Many women behaving like this would still, unfortunately, be condemned by society and few husbands would understand.

In a sense all menstruating women go through a kind of mini rite of passage every time they have a period. The time building up to the period is a time of heightened sensitivity, when strong feelings are around. This is the red time, the passionate time, the time of hysteria, the time of Dionysus. It can be a dangerous time when women may rage and even appear to go mad for a while. All the niceness, order and control that they may usually exhibit goes out of the window. Dionysus has called them. They do perhaps need to let themselves run with him, go with the flow, let all the feelings

Figure 19.   Womb Mysteries, 1987

out, live and enjoy them. If they don't, then 'madness' is more likely to strike. It is a time of going right down into the depths of the instincts, whether these be anger, sorrow or joy. Many women are highly sexual at this time too. And then the blood begins to flow. There is a letting go, just like in the mysteries. There is a sacrifice and a release at the same time. Within days a new calm has usually set in and a different kind of energy builds up to another high point mid-cycle at ovulation, when sexual and creative energy is often at a peak. We have dipped down into the darkness and then reached back up to the heights. Neither phase is better or worse than the other. Both are needed. Letting out the blood serves as a transition from one to the other.

Indeed, the menstrual cycle could be seen as the prototype for all other kinds of rite of passage. As our bodies are the place in which we experience nature most directly, they are the site of our sacred link with the goddess as nature. Each month women go through a kind of dying and rebirth, just as nature does with its seasons and phases of the moon. Menstruation used to be seen as a time when women were more powerful, and its links with the moon must have seemed magical. There within our own bodies are the most powerful mysteries of all.

Utopian Visions

What would a society based on natural laws, rhythms and cycles, rather than competition and hierarchies, actually be like? How would it feel if love was more than a nice idea, and was instead an energy that was understood and used in all its many forms by everyone as a prime motivation in life, rather than for power over others? How would it be to live in a society in constant flux where change was fully accepted and expected, where uncertainty could be enjoyed and where 'going with the flow' was as natural as being in control?

It is hard to imagine such a society and perhaps even harder to imagine how we might get from here to there. Yet under the surface of today's chaos a new way is preparing to be born. It seems to be manifesting in hundreds of different forms that might at first appear to have no connections with each other. In this part of the book I am going to fantasize that all these trends go further and further over a period of about 500 years and imagine what a society based on a different, more rhythmic, non-hierarchical way of thinking could be like.

The essential features differing such a society from our own would be as follows:

1. The underlying model of thought in every aspect of life would be the interconnection of opposites and the idea of having *both* one side *and* the other. Society would not be

based on *either/or* thinking in which one side has to win.
This new way of thinking is becoming increasingly
common in new age, feminist and even business circles.
The implications are actually nothing short of revolutionary. Our whole Western civilization has been built up
on hierarchical frameworks and opposites divided into
good and bad, superior and inferior, male and female, light
and dark, mind and body, and so on. Everything from
religion to economics has been affected by this model. An
alternative one of equally valued differences, through
which life flows and changes, is just as valid and possible
for our brains to conceive. Western dualism is not
biologically inherited.

2. It would be a highly psychological sophisticated society.
Basic human needs, from the physical to the spiritual,
would be accepted and understood. They, rather than
purely economic considerations, would be the basis for
social organizations. Children would become psychologically literate at an early age. Perhaps everyone would
have counselling or therapy of some kind at certain times
of their lives and it would not be seen as anything out of
the ordinary or embarrassing. Already today more and
more newspapers, magazines and television shows are
using the language of psychology. It is no longer only the
highly educated who talk about complexes, neurosis or
relating present problems to childhood relationships.

3. The spirituality of such a society would be based on
nature, with people free to choose their own symbols and
myths and religions. Love would be seen as the main
spiritual energy of the universe and not as made available
only through a figure like Christ or particular practices.
Perhaps the main mythical figures would be a goddess and
her consort, to help preserve sexual balance in the society.
Women and men would, of course, be seen as profoundly
equal, but a goddess deity to represent the love energy or
nature or the life force might ensure that the female side
of life is properly respected and as powerful as the male.

Rhythm and balance would be the underlying forces in society, as they are in nature. People would be constantly striving for balance of both inner and outer kinds. As perfect balance is unachievable, striving towards it would continue to be a part of life.

4. Equality would be another guiding principle. Again, people would be constantly striving for equality, which is also a kind of balance. At the same time differences would be celebrated; it would be a pluralistic society with enormous diversity in every aspect of life. People would not look down on (or up to) others for being different. With better psychological understanding people would be able to see why they 'need' enemies or scapegoats or to feel superior. These 'needs' can then either be lost altogether as people feel whole, satisfied and important, or expressed symbolically, through rituals for example. Already this kind of exploration of why and how groups come to hate each other is happening around the world, as the inner world of psychological experience is seen to be related to the outer world of politics and war. It is still only a tiny minority of people who are thinking this way, but their numbers are growing.

5. Children would be seen as very special and would perhaps be a relative rarity. People would no longer be expected automatically to have children because they were married or of a certain age. Indeed, marriage itself might very well die out, and there would be a wide variety of social, sexual and family arrangements. There would have to be particular provisions for children, with extensive parent training and certain commitments to ensure stability. Today's nuclear family might well be only one out of many kinds of groups in which children are brought up. Small groups of same or different-sexed adults might commit themselves to a child and be its family, whether biologically connected or not. Already we can see this trend, in that people no longer feel so much pressure, in the West at least, to have children just because it is expected

of them. There are also more gays and lesbians parenting children, and more single parents, some of whom get together in shared households. There are even groups of people of different ages who form themselves into their own chosen families. All of these alternative arrangements are slowly becoming more acceptable in the West, and families made up of stepchildren from serial marriages are increasingly common in society as a whole. There is an awareness now that bringing up children and sexual relationships don't automatically go together in the way that the modern social myth has decreed, and we do not all have to 'fall in love, get married and have babies'.

6. In economics and politics the equal valuing of opposites would also apply. A society dedicated to equality would have to have some central control, perhaps even as far as providing basic physical necessities in return for certain work contributions by those who are able. But free enterprise would also be needed for those who chose it. This mixed economy is already developing in the West, especially in Europe. Another pair of equal opposites are centralization and decentralization. Both are needed for different purposes. Centralization can ensure equality and provide solutions for widespread problems, while decentralization helps people feel more important and in control of their own affairs. Individualism and collectivism are also both needed. Where there has been an imbalance, as in the recent over-emphasis on the individual, there may need to be a swing in the opposite direction, in this case towards greater collectivity. This striving to balance the opposites can go on at all levels and in all aspects of politics and economics. There would also need to be a constant balancing of human needs and the needs of nature, to keep the planet alive. With a spirituality based on reverence for nature, there would be powerful motivation to work *with* rather than against nature. After all, we are a part of her too. This green consciousness is growing fast everywhere and is already no longer a minority interest.

7. Current Western standards of living would have to be drastically cut. There would be a sense of all peoples being both planetary citizens *and* part of their own communities. The first and third worlds would become more inter-connected and equal, learning from each other and sharing economically. Already there is an increase in respect for native traditions among many Westerners, but they haven't yet been asked to give up their cars! The world economy would be less and less based on the car and on the expectation of endless economic growth. Increasingly sophisticated and complex technology would be less important than technology that is appropriate to human and planetary needs. Indeed, the whole goal-seeking, one-directional pursuit of progress would no longer be relevant. Snakes rather than ladders would be the symbols of the future. Change would be seen as a flowing in and out, backwards and forwards, as part of the various balancing processes going on throughout society and nature, not as a single movement from point A to point B. This model of change is far more in keeping with the natural processes of earth. Already green parties are arguing for a no-growth economic system. Already scientists, businessmen and others are using different criteria for evaluating their work, criteria based more on human need or environmental concerns than on the pursuit of profit or power, or on the making of things simply because they can be made, however useless or destructive they may be. Already the consumer movement is making demands based on these different criteria. Health is a major issue in this respect. People are respecting and caring for their bodies more, learning more about the various balancing mechanisms in the human body. Alternative medicine is already based on the rhythmic model of opposites needing to be balanced: yin and yang, balancing the elements of earth, air, fire and water, unblocking energy flows, and so on, are everyday concepts for the increasing number of people who now use alternative medicine.

Around the world millions of people are struggling to redress economic and social imbalances, such as those between women and men, black and white, and rich and poor. It's all part of the same process of moving towards a more equal and balanced society, a process that will no doubt continue for the rest of human history. For, paradoxically, the perfectly balanced society would be dead, like anything else permanently balanced. Most Utopias have a dead and final feel to them. They are stagnant in their very perfection. Our vision for the future needs to be one of constant change, of striving for equality and balance while recognizing its impossibility as any 'final' solution.

From Here to There: a Fantasy

So how might we make the transition to a society based on natural laws and rhythms? I like to imagine a gradual collapse of patriarchy and capitalism as the world economic order crumbles and social and family structures move away from male dominance and hierarchy. There may, however, be natural disasters or wars first to speed up the process.

Imagine that the car industry collapses first, with world-wide consequences such as an increasing emphasis on small-scale industry for local needs and less need for mobility. The nation states could all break up into smaller areas that are self-governing, with some centralization remaining both at world and continent level.

I like to imagine that the major patriarchal religions will gradually transform, putting more and more emphasis on the female aspect and on nature, until a new, nature-based spirituality emerges everywhere. Again, there may be bloody battles first. It may not be too hard to transform the Virgin Mary back into the 'great goddess', or even Allah into the 'feminine' principle of nature, or to reclaim Lilith for the Judaic tradition; but to fully transform male religious power will take a massive shift in consciousness and a surrender to whatever is conceived of as goddess. Yet a new spiritual awareness is vital for the new society to develop. Without it the degree of uncertainty experienced by people would be too great and they would revert to the old securities. And as we have seen in this book, central religious myths such as god being an old man in the sky have profound and far-reaching negative effects on the rest of society. I like to imagine that such a transformation of consciousness will happen quite quickly, as some proponents of new-age ideas believe, but it may take at least 500 years. Men, male gods and male competitive consciousness have already dominated human cultures for 5,000 years and this is not going to change overnight.

With the new spirituality, differing religions and ethnic backgrounds would become less and less important as sources of conflict. The goddess loves everyone. People would continue to express and be proud of whatever identities they chose or were born with, but without any sense of superiority or inferiority, as such hierarchical thinking would have largely disappeared.

To change people's model of thinking would not require state-controlled programmes of education, just a different spiritual mythology that would be naturally passed on from parents to children. Since the rhythm model is so much closer to nature, as manifested for example in the vegetation cycle and the moon cycle, it would make sense to children because they would see it in action. While *some* competition for adult attention and care in childhood is probably inevitable, children who are deeply wanted and surrounded by love as well as firm boundaries are less likely to fight others for what they are not getting, which is usually love. And if, as they acquire language and thought, the models they learn are all based on equality and the balancing of opposites, their behaviour will be affected. It is likely to differ from that of people brought up on competition and either/or thinking. What may happen is a deep shift in consciousness from hierarchical to rhythmic thinking.

I can imagine feminism growing and deepening all over the

world and bringing about changes at all levels of society. There will probably be massive backlashes and times when women are put right down again, but eventually the power of the female side of life, with its different models of being and thinking, will come into its own. Indeed it will be when women have control over their own bodies and their own sexuality that the birth rate will slow down, provided that the old patriarchal religious attitudes towards women have been transformed too. This will have a profound effect on population growth and give the human race a better chance of surviving.

I have mentioned here just some of the changes that might take place. Many groups and individuals are already moving in this direction, including all those involved in alternative medicine, Paganism, egalitarian politics, whether at local or national levels, the green movement, and so on. It is in these movements and trends that we can see the seeds of an emerging new society.

In the Year 2500

Imagine waking up one morning in a totally different kind of society. How would it feel? What would you be doing? What would you like it to be like? Everyone would answer these questions differently. Perhaps we all need to have a go at creating our own personal visions, not least because they can give us courage and hope when the present gets tough. Here is my personal vision.

I wake up in the arms of my current lover and make love slowly for at least two hours as two equal, powerful, sexual adults. As a man he does not need to be always in control or to dominate. In this society the arts and spirituality of sex are taken very seriously and play a major role in life. We adore each other's bodies as incarnations of goddess and god and spend time first centring ourselves and building up the energy within us and between us. But he does not live with me. Even though we spend most nights together I need to have some time alone.

I live in a villa-type house with a central courtyard full of plants, flowers and running water. Architecture has changed dramatically. And without cars around, roads do not dictate everything as they once did. Homes blend more into the landscape and are more rounded and flowing. People are involved in designing their own homes, so there is little uniformity. To the twentieth-century person it would all seem rather messy and higgledy-piggledy. There are lots of market gardens in between the homes.

Most people live with others, in family groups chosen personally. There are contracts of commitment to staying together for certain periods of time, such as seven years, as people need to belong and feel secure. The home is provided by local government. Everyone has one big room of their own and there are also several shared rooms. Those who choose to be involved with private enterprise can build more rooms of their own in addition to what they have a right to. Each home has a shared meditation room and another room for meetings. Regular discussions about home issues are held, sometimes with an outside counsellor. Most people have their own personal counsellor too.

Personally I have chosen to commit myself to living with people who are not my lovers: two men and three women. They are compatible with me in other ways. We have also decided to take on a child, biologically one of the women's. But we are all 'parents' to that child and take on appropriate commitments to it. At the age of seven and then again at around 14 a child can choose to change its parents if it wants. And some of the 'parents' agree to longer commitments than others. But each child expects to have at least three adults committed to it for a lifetime, although they do not necessarily live with him or her after the age of 14.

In our home people each have their own small kitchen and then share a big communal one for most meals. So when I get up, I have breakfast in my room, remembering of course to give thanks to the goddess first. More important than *what* I eat is the feeling of gratitude to the earth *while* I eat.

In my fantasy everything is warm. Technology has advanced in some areas to change climates and to give indoor and outdoor 'central heating'. Enormous bubbles are stretched over wide areas to keep in the warmth, so it's like living in giant greenhouses. My clothes can therefore be light and comfortable.

I then go to the studio I share with two other artists, five minutes walk away through the trees. My art work is part of the 'free' economy, an activity I do in my own time and make money at if I choose. I also have a job as a counsellor, which is my contribution to the society.

Everyone has to work a certain number of days in a year, or hours per week, to contribute to the community in exchange for benefits such as housing. Such work is found for everyone with a great deal of counselling and soul searching. Most people are found something that they can love doing, but if not there are certain compensations, such as fewer hours. Young people are given plenty of opportunity to learn from adults in all areas of work and to try out as much as possible. Indeed this 'apprenticeship' is the most important aspect of education. They can also choose which individual adults to learn from so that they do not have to be taught by teachers whom they don't like.

Reading, writing and arithmetic are less important, as the main forms of communication are verbal, telepathic or very high tech, such as video phones. Books are still available, and people still write them, but only a few people are interested in them, as museum items. All the old emphasis on the written word and the law is gone. Common law is the only one that still applies. And people prefer to tell each other stories than read them, and to talk face to face rather than write letters. Children instead learn a great deal about psychology and human communication of the more direct kinds. They are told lots of stories about the goddess and her consort, none of which are sexist. They spend time with their own age groups playing, being creative and learning about relationships. But they also spend more time in groups of mixed ages than most children used to. The opposites of control and letting go are important. The children have clear boundaries and learn to respect others, but there are special times for letting go too. Adults also have such 'free' times, perhaps going to the playroom just to mess about with the kids. And there are lots of festivals and organized wildness as the seasons change and at full moons.

Every community has people playing the roles of priestesses and priests who organize rituals both at significant times in the calendar and for any important events in people's lives. The people concerned are often involved in designing such rituals. Most people have rituals for all important events in their lives, such as moving home, changing jobs, starting and ending relationships, and, of course, there are rites of passage at appropriate times in a person's life, such as puberty. As with every other occupation, children are trained up to become priestesses or priests. And as with everything else, this job is not seen as higher or better than any other. All work has equal status. People who choose to do their bit of extra money-making on the side are not seen as superior either, even if they do have more rooms in their house. In fact such people tend to be pitied, as it is clear that they are not easily satisfied.

Love and self-fulfilment are seen as far more important than money. Many people's needs are met without their making or spending money at all. As far as possible each community grows most of its own food and manufactures whatever goods it needs. People lead much simpler lives on the whole, and stay for much of their lives in the same community. Any travelling is on centrally provided trains, boats and possibly occasional aeroplanes. There are, however, high tech communications systems joining up areas across the world. Computers do a lot of the work now done in offices to collect and distribute information. People do not feel isolated in their communities, and as their lives at home are so much more satisfying and exciting there is less need to travel. Most communities have a mixture of races and types of people, although there are some people who prefer to live only with their own kind. Women's communities, black communities and gay communities still exist, but there is less need for them without the hierarchical thinking that used to dominate society.

After spending a few hours painting I go to meet a woman friend for lunch at one of the private eating places set up by an enterprising couple of teenagers who weren't happy with the restrictions on clothes purchase from the community. It's the job of a number of community members to spend about 30 weeks of the year designing and making clothes for the community, preferably with the co-operation of the people who are going to wear them. As their skills are limited, private shops also sell clothes imported from elsewhere and made with more style. In order to buy such clothes, people need to have money, which they have to earn, so these two boys opened their own restaurant with a bit of help from the community market garden and the provision of a house that was empty. I talk to my friend about the pros and cons of selling my paintings and also about problems in my relationship with my lover or a housemate. Such problems will never go away, but at least in this psychologically sophisticated society there is ample opportunity to sort them out honestly. I also go to a squash court to get rid of my anger, because feelings won't have disappeared either.

Then I visit my own counsellor before going on to do my four hours a day counselling others. In addition to regular counselling there are also places that people can go to when depressed or going through difficult transition periods. These are loving, beautiful places for 'time out' from normal life. There are healing centres in which all kinds of methods are used, and high tech, hospital techniques are available when appropriate. The equipment for this will have been imported from specialist factories in exchange for something this particular community specialises in. Each community has its specialism.

Communities vary in size, but are usually several thousand strong, with maybe smaller groupings of homes into 'villages'.

Each community has a healing and spiritual centre, a leisure centre, a cultural centre, a communications computer centre, and shops both private and public. The public ones, of course, ration everything according to fairly basic needs. I am given around 5 lbs of potatoes a week, but if I want more I can sell a painting and buy more at a private shop. The constant tension between private and public is a feature of community life. Each village area has its representative and there are also various specialist representatives, such as the priestess, to meet regularly and look at problems. There are also magistrates' courts of a kind, but with an emphasis on common law, punishments that are intended to help victims, and lots of mediation and negotiation. There is much public debate on important issues, and referendums are held to make specific decisions. Everyone over the age of seven can take part, and even the younger children can have their say: such debating provides an important part of children's education. There are still specialist schools for specialist skills such as medical surgery, but most people learn any skills they need from close observation of people already practising.

Play centres are available in every community, with organized programmes for children and adults, and space for 'free expression'. Young children are generally supervised, often by older children, and the rules of the place are negotiated, agreed and kept to. But these centres feel totally different from schools as they used to be, as the emphasis is on child-centred, self-directed learning, the importance of play and creativity, and on adults returning to learn. There is no particular emphasis on the written word, and computers are used instead of books to store information.

Creative writing, story telling and poetry are shared a lot at the play centres, at rituals and festivals and just about everywhere. People do not feel much need to preserve things for ever, or to compete with others to be the best for ever. Indeed nothing is seen as for ever. All creativity is enjoyed in the present as a part of everyday life. Objects made can be easily discarded when no longer needed. It is the process of making them and their immediate uses and relevance to the group that give them value. All creative activities are seen as equally important. Art is not just paintings or sculptures, but includes cooking as well. Doing things with love and concentration is more important than producing perfect products.

My day now continues with my other work, my contribution to the community, which is counselling. I do not see any of the jobs I do as superior or inferior to any others. They are just what I do. My identity is not dependent on them. From an early age we are encouraged to explore spiritual truths around such questions as 'Who am I?' Children are moulded as little as possible into one particular type of personality. People are acknowledged to have many sides and many personalities but also an essential core, which is their deep self and which has no gender or personality, but is part of the great love of the universe, the great rhythms of nature, the goddess.

I have a room in the healing/temple complex for my work. I have 10 people whom I see regularly. Almost everyone in the community has a counsellor of their own. Different arrangements suit different people. Some come once a week, others only in times of crisis. But it is thought important to have someone to talk to outside the usual group of friends, home group or work colleagues. There are also groups for exploring general issues and for particular problems such as phobias. These may be self-help or led by a counsellor.

After I have seen my three people for the day I go into one of the temple rooms for some quiet meditation and contact with the goddess, both to relax and to ask for guidance. There are many different kinds of temple rooms catering to differing ideas and needs for the divine. The one I go to is a very colourful room with lots of candles and richly embroidered drapes. Other rooms are more simple and plain. For me there is a need to have strong visual images and an atmosphere of sensuality. The statues in my temple room are of an enormous Earth mother with massive thighs and large breasts, sitting

Figure 20.   Dreaming, 1984

behind an altar, half hidden with drapes. On either side of the altar sit a woman, sensual and strong, and a man, beautiful, gentle and powerful. There is also a pool of water into which people can dip to cleanse themselves. Any symbolic sacrifice can be left on the altar. The priestess is available most of the time, either to perform an individual ritual or to talk to people. I just need a quiet time.

Later I go home to share a communal meal with other members of my house. We take turns in providing these communal meals about once a week. Some home groups have them every night, but we have chosen each other because we like to be on our own a lot, while still needing people. Afterwards I go dancing at the leisure centre with my lover and other friends, have a go on the drums that I'm learning to play, stay up too late and end up back at my lover's place, falling asleep the minute I put my head down.

Poems

Return of the Goddess

Long before the dawn of time,
When I was strong, secure and wise,
The earth, the stars, all love was mine.
Then one day
I bore a son divine.

A golden child, a magic boy,
My sun, my moon, my favourite toy.
He stayed with me through life and death,
Connected by a cord of flesh.
A part of me he lived inside.

At first there was no hate or pride,
Just warmth and joy and lots of play.
Then out he came as form, as clay,
And grew and grew, as big as man,
Turned round on me with eyes of fear,
As only human children can.

My power became a major care.
He fought me hard
To make me small,
And weak and soft,
While he felt tall.

The cord of flesh still held us bound;
I loved too much to let him go
Till I was buried in the ground;
My streams and rivers ceased to flow.

I could not breathe, I could not sing,
It seemed I'd lost almost everything,
But knew the cord must now be cut,
To give me back my power, my life,
And let me rise out of the mud.
I could no longer be a 'wife'.

So I took the axe of ancient rites,
And slashed in two the cord of love,
With pain and tears and even fright.
The blood poured out
And out and out,
A sea of red flowed all about.

At last I turned away in peace,
And saw the light of sun and sea,
A love more wide that couldn't cease,
To fill my world and let me be —
Myself.

1992

The Moon is in My Belly

The moon is in my belly,
White cool glow,
In the deep below.

Ripening readiness,
Rounding down,
Earth bound.

New-found interiors,
Secret blood truth,
Holy chambers glowing.

Black waves swelling,
Snake waters flowing
Through dark crevices into
The dreaming pregnant tombs.

1990

Rebirth of Eros
(A feminist trying to reconnect with men)

Dark sun of some ancient sacrifice,
Let your green-cool, coal-black piercing eyes
Gorge through my unprotected heart,
Burn in my unfolded flesh.
Die again in me.
Cry on the stones, cry on the sea,
Cry for the lost boys,
Of the vengeful furies' cause.

Let me cradle your bones
To enable your soul
To come home.

From out of the sea,
Where your mother was lost,
Great Aphrodite.

(For my friend from Lemnos where Greek
myth tells us the women once killed off all
the men and boys.)

1990

Isis's Lament for Osiris

I remember when long ago I lost you
Down the wide green river of forgotten time,
Into the sea of eternal blue,
Young god who once was mine.

For five thousand years
The angry fathers ruled,
Ignoring my tears,
Being deaf to my fears,
Imprisoned my children in schools.

They broke you into many pieces,
Divided head from heart,
And then they finally split off sex
From all the other parts.

But now their world is crumbling
And our time at last is coming.

I sometimes think I've found you,
My long lost lover/son,
Then bits of you go missing
And the mourning still goes on.

I cover you with kisses
To heal the ancient wounds,
Yet my love too often misses
The heart that I have found.

Can I bear to be strong and steady
And wait a little longer,
Till you are whole and ready.

1991

At the Centre of the Labyrinth

From natural caves of eternal beginnings
To the conscious labyrinth life keeps bringing.
Following Ariadne's golden string,
Product of my own imagining.
The myth turned real,
Began to feel
Entwined, enmeshed in twisted threads,
Of long-forgotten fatal dreads.

The winding streets of Naxos town
Led to Dionysus' starry crown.
His bed of passion and letting down,
Irrational,
Unrationed bliss,
Finally found.

Still place of foetal ecstasy to mend,
At the centre,
Round the bend.
It was the end.

1990

Earth Mysteries

The night my waiting ended,
It felt like he was dead.
One ritual year gone by,
Since first we lay beneath the sky.
Beside the well,
Below the cave,
On ancient land,
His spirit saved.

My body earth grown dry,
Received at last warm rain.
And deep inside the stifled cry,
Of old new love, new hope, new pain.
Turned into song,
The beat of drum,
A faster pulse,
The call to come.

It finished slowly, in silence,
Leaving behind,
A richer soil,
In balance.

1990

Further reading

Bachofen, J. J., *Myth, Religion and Mother Right,* Princeton University Press, Princeton, New Jersey, 1967.

Baring, Anne and Cashford, Jules, *The Myth of the Goddess,* Viking Arkana (Penguin), London, 1991.

Bayley, Harold, *The Lost Language of London,* Jonathan Cape, London, 1935.

Bolen, Jean, *Goddesses in Everywoman,* Harper & Row, New York, 1984

—— *Gods in Everyman,* Harper & Row, New York, 1986.

Chaplin, Jocelyn, *Feminist Counselling in Action,* Sage, London, 1988.

Dworkin, Andrea, *Pornography: Men Possessing Women,* The Women's Press, London, 1984.

Eisler, Riane, *The Chalice and the Blade,* Unwin Hyman, London, 1990.

Fierz-David, Linda, *Women's Dionysian Initiation: The Villa of Mysteries in Pompeii,* Spring Publications, Dallas, 1988.

Friedrich, Paul, *The Meaning of Aphrodite,* University of Chicago Press, Chicago, 1978.

Fromm, Erich, *The Art of Loving,* Unwin Hyman, London, 1957.

Gadon, Elinor W., *The Once and Future Goddess,* Harper & Row, New York, 1989; the Aquarian Press, London, 1990.

Gimbutas, Marija, *Goddesses and Gods of Old Europe,* Thames & Hudson, London, 1974.

8

Goodison, Lucy, *Moving Heaven and Earth,* The Women's Press, London, 1990.

Graves, Robert, *The Greek Myths, Vols. 1 and 2,* Penguin, UK, 1955.

Hall, Nor, *The Moon and the Virgin,* The Women's Press, London, 1980.

—— *Those Women,* Spring Publications, Dallas, 1988.

Hite, Shere, *The Hite Report on Women and Love,* Pandora Press, London, 1989.

Kerenyi, C., *Dionysus,* Routledge & Kegan Paul, London, 1976.

Matthews, Caitlín, *The Elements of the Goddess,* Element, Shaftesbury, 1989.

Matthews, Caitlín (ed.), *Voices of the Goddess,* Thorsons, London, 1990.

Norwood, Robin, *Women Who Love Too Much,* Arrow Books, London, 1986.

Perera, Sylvia Brinton, *Descent to the Goddess: A Way of Initiation for Women,* Inner City Books, Toronto, 1981.

Potter, Chesca and Munro, Caroline, *Elen, Goddess of Nature,* Spiral Press Publications, Oxford, 1986.

Rowan, John, *The Horned God,* Routledge & Kegan Paul, London, 1987.

Sjöö, Monica and Mor, Barbara, *The Ancient Religion of the Great Cosmic Mother of All,* The Rainbow Press, Trondheim, 1981.

Starhawk, *Dreaming the Dark: Magic, Sex and Politics,* Beacon Press, Boston, 1982 and 1988; Unwin Hyman, London, 1990.

Stone, Merlin, *When God was a Woman,* Harvest, The Dial Press, San Diego, 1976.

Teish, Luisah, *Jambalaya,* Harper & Row, New York, 1988.

Walker, Barbara, *The Women's Encyclopaedia of Myths and Secrets,* Harper & Row, New York, 1983.

Whitmont, Edward, *Return of the Goddess,* Arkana, Routledge & Kegan Paul, London, 1987.

Wolf, Naomi, *The Beauty Myth*, Vintage, London, 1991.

Wombwell, Felicity, *The Goddess Changes,* Mandala, HarperCollins, London, 1991.

Woodman, Marion, *The Pregnant Virgin,* Inner City Books, Toronto, 1985.

THE PILLAR OF ISIS

*A Practical Manual on the
Mysteries of the Goddess*

VIVIENNE O'REGAN

The Pillar of Isis is a revolutionary new guide which allows you to experience the path of the Goddess: a path of positive union on all levels, including healing our relationship with others and with the Earth herself.

The combination of theory and practice eases the reader into an active, personal relationship with the Goddess in her various forms, and provides a complete course of development from basic skills to more advanced techniques of meditation, visualisation and ritual. Progressive creative visualisation techniques guide the reader to make individual contact with the Inner Temple of Isis: a place of teaching and a repository of her love and wisdom. The key to the Goddess mysteries is to 'know thyself'. Exercises in gentle self-exploration serve to balance the energies contacted through the main meditational sequences and aid the reader in coming to a better rapport with those about us and with the world we inhabit.

In Part Two the author examines the synthesis of the Pillar and its temples with the Kabalah, Tarot, chakras and auras, and gives guidance for further work on the Pillar for those wishing to enter into training for ordination.

Vivienne O'Regan has studied esoteric and psychological disciplines for twenty years. She is the founder and facilitator of a teaching centre within the Fellowship of Isis, of which she is an ordained Priestess. *The Pillar of Isis* is the culmination of her courses of meditation on the Goddess.

JOURNEY OF THE PRIESTESS

*A Journey of Spiritual Awakening
and Empowerment*

ASIA SHEPSUT

The issue of female priesthood has moved to the forefront of public debate within the Christian Church. Yet many influential women working outside orthodox religion are already operating as priestesses, often at a very high level. This book traces the remains of a submerged tradition of priestesses, whose characteristics have remained constant for millennia.

In the ancient world, throughout the rise and fall of great civilizations, women held great power. Their influence gradually spread westwards until it finally took root in Greece and Rome. By examining history, ancient stories and images, Asia Shepsut links age-old ritual to modern conditions. The worship of Inanna, Ishtar, Astarte, Isis, Athena and Aphrodite, with the yearly cycle of festivals and the celebration of the sacred marriage, still has striking relevance for today's priestess striving to blend everyday life with spiritual service.

Women still have much to learn about reclaiming their spiritual powers. Through drawing on the mythological cycle of life and death, with its interplay between male and female energies, women can become contemporary priestesses. It is a unique opportunity to create a rebalancing of the sexes, and lay the foundations of a common spiritual practice.

Asia Shepsut is an art historian and archaeologist. She has travelled widely in the Middle East, where she carried out much of the research for this book. She has co-authored and edited several books, including *The Year of the Goddess*.

SOPHIA – GODDESS OF WISDOM

*The Divine Feminine from
Black Goddess to World-Soul*

CAITLÍN MATTHEWS

Sophia – Goddess of Wisdom takes the reader on a journey through time, seeking out the presence of the Goddess from pre-Christian spirituality to the present day. Drawing mainly on sources from the Western tradition, the many faces of the Goddess are revealed. She is shown as the primeval Black Goddess of the earth, as Saviour Goddess, the Gnostic Sophia, World-Soul, Apocalyptic Virgin and as the Mother of God. We see how the foundation mysteries of the Goddess underlie the esoteric streams of orthodox religions, and trace her hermetic presence in Qabala and alchemy. Finally, we track her appearance in the realms of Goddess religion, feminist theology and the New Age Movement.

This definitive work gives Sophia a voice that will be welcomed by all who seek to reaffirm the Goddess as the central pivot of creation and as the giver of practical and spiritual wisdom.

Caitlín Matthews has written nearly twenty books on many aspects of Western Spirituality. As an ordained priestess in the Fellowship of Isis, she offers a non-denominational ministry to people in need. She is married to the author John Matthews, with whom she has written and taught worldwide.

MOVING HEAVEN AND EARTH

*Sexuality, Spirituality
and Social Change*

LUCY GOODISON

The West, according to this original and profoundly important book, has inherited a divided world view based on the splitting of mind from body and spirit from matter. Our language and symbols reflect this division, and we think in pairs of opposites: male/female, white/black, active/passive, in ways which reinforce conformist and often oppressive stereotypes.

Moving Heaven and Earth argues that symbols are not god-given but man-made and can be changed. Goodison's own research into ancient Crete revealed a holistic, woman-centred culture. Alternative esoteric symbolism such as astrology and Tarot can also help us discover and create an integrated spirituality.

Goodison offers practical exercises drawn from psychotherapy and meditation to enable individuals to develop different symbolic vocabularies and challenge the mind/body split in their own lives.

Lucy Goodison is a writer, lecturer and therapist. She is co-author of the best selling therapy book *In Our Own Hands*.

in LOVE IN AN AGE OF UNCERTAINTY

THE PILLAR OF ISIS	1 85538 236 9	£9.99	☐
JOURNEY OF THE PRIESTESS	1 85538 282 2	£12.99	☐
SOPHIA – GODDESS OF WISDOM	1 85538 275 X	£9.99	☐
MOVING HEAVEN AND EARTH	0 04 440861 7	£8.99	☐
DAUGHTERS OF EVE	0 85030 977 8	£7.99	☐
THE HERO AND THE GODDESS	1 85538 285 7	£9.99	☐

All these books are available from your local bookseller or can be ordered direct from the publishers.

To order direct just tick the titles you want and fill in the form below:

Name:_____

Address: _____

_____

_____ Postcode: _____

Send to: Thorsons Mail Order, Dept 3, HarperCollins*Publishers*, Westerhill Road, Bishopbriggs, Glasgow G64 2QT.
Please enclose a cheque or postal order or your authority to debit your Visa/Access account —

Credit card no:_____

Expiry date: _____

Signature: _____

— up to the value of the cover price plus:
UK & BFPO: Add £1.00 for the first book and 25p for each additional book ordered.
Overseas orders including Eire: Please add £2.95 service charge. Books will be sent by surface mail but quotes for airmail despatches will be given on request.

24 HOUR TELEPHONE ORDERING SERVICE FOR ACCESS/VISA CARDHOLDERS — TEL: **041 772 2281.**